LISTENING
PAYS

ACHIEVE SIGNIFICANCE
THROUGH THE POWER OF LISTENING

RICK BOMMELJE

Leadership & Listening
Institute

ISBN 13: 978-0-9883076-0-5
ISBN 13: 978-0-9883076-1-2 (e-book)

Library of Congress Control Number: 2012916773

Cover and interior design by James Monroe Design, LLC.

Printed in the United States of America
HCI Printing & Publishing

First Printing: 2013

17 16 15 14 13   5 4 3 2 1

Leadership & Listening
Institute

8530 Amber Oak Dr.
Orlando, FL 32817
(407) 679-7280
www.listeningpays.com

To order, visit www.listeningpays.com

To my precious wife and soul mate, Quin,
who has taught me through her consistent and impactful
actions during the past four decades how much listening
pays in every area of life.

CONTENTS

Foreword . . . . *vii*

Acknowledgements . . . . *xi*

Prologue . . . . *xiii*

Chapter 1
The Writing on the Wall 1

Chapter 2
The Ultimatum 11

Chapter 3
Close Call 25

Chapter 4
A New Day Dawns 35

Chapter 5
Listening Is a Gift 47

Chapter 6
Maturity Gap 57

Chapter 7
Trouble at Home 65

Chapter 8
Build a Solid Foundation 73

Chapter 9
SIER* 87

v

Chapter 10
The Path to Awareness. 97

Chapter 11
Relationships Matter 107

Chapter 12
Develop Healthy Habits. 115

Chapter 13
Restarting 129

Chapter 14
Take 100% Responsibility. 143

Chapter 15
Ditch the Distractions 167

Chapter 16
Lead Your Emotions 187

Chapter 17
Take Meaningful Action 205

Epilogue *229*

Endnotes. *235*

About Rick Bommelje *237*

Meet The "Real" Alfred *239*

Meet The "Real" Dr. Grove *241*

Listening Pays Resources *243*

Foreword
by Marshall Goldsmith

Listening Pays. Its title could not more aptly describe the lesson taught in this leadership novel by Rick Bommelje. With story and example, Rick provides us with answers to two significant questions: What is a good listener? And, if you aren't a good listener, how do you become one?

For me, one of the most poignant moments in the book is when Stu, the main character of the story, asks his boss if there is anything specific he should focus on to improve his performance. The boss responds clearly that Stu needs to be a better listener. Stu asks again, hoping for an answer that will help him. To the boss and to the reader, this is a perfect example of someone who doesn't listen. And, like most of us would, the boss gets frustrated. He tells Stu that he's just told him everything he needs to know to be successful, and promptly asks him to leave his office.

Stu thinks he's being a good listener and is confused. And, like Stu, you may think you're a pretty good listener.

But do the people around you agree? Has anyone ever looked at you with a disappointed expression and said, "Are you listening?" My guess is the answer is *yes*. Have you ever then replied to the person in an annoyed voice, "What do you mean, am I listening?" and then repeated what he or she said verbatim—to prove they were wrong? My guess is again, *yes*.

And just one more question: Did your annoyed response dramatically improve your relationship with that other human being? My guess this time is a resounding "No!"

In *Listening Pays*, Rick provides solutions to help you become a better listener and achieve significance. He also shows you what it looks like when you're not a good listener. Simple things help, like apologizing for not listening and showing that you really care when someone else is speaking. Try it the next time someone looks at you and says, "You're not listening." Apologize by saying, "I am sorry. I will try to do better in the future."

Here are a few more listening tactics for your inter-personal encounters:

- Don't interrupt.

- Don't finish the other person's sentences.

- Don't say, "I knew that."

If you can do these things while you're in a conversation, you will inevitably find that the other person will think you are a great person.

In *Listening Pays,* Rick will teach you how you can do these things to show that you are listening. Read this book and take action on what it teaches you. You will be glad you did!

Life is good.
Marshall Goldsmith

Marshall Goldsmith was recently recognized as the world's most influential leadership thinker in the bi-annual *Thinkers50* study sponsored by the *Harvard Business Review.* His thirty-one books include the *New York Times* bestsellers *MOJO* and *What Got You Here Won't Get You There.*

ACKNOWLEDGEMENTS

It took five years for *Listening Pays* to be birthed. After multiple editions and "do-overs," I owe a debt of gratitude to many kindred spirits who assisted me during this fascinating journey.

I am forever indebted to Dr. Lyman (Manny) K. Steil, the foremost authority on Listening in the corporate world. For twenty-five years, Manny has been my Listening mentor, friend, colleague, and co-author of the pioneering book *Listening Leaders*. Much of the inspiration for the creation of *Listening Pays* has come directly from our foundational work on listening leadership. Manny coined the expression "Listening pays in many ways" decades ago and through his exceptional work has taught leaders at all levels the profound impact that listening has in their lives.

I am grateful to Alfred Marino, whose life has been the inspiration for the character Alfred Damato. Alfred's tremendous spirit is contagious and embodies the essence of listening as a way of being.

I am greatly appreciative of Dr. Marshall Goldsmith, who authored the foreword. Marshall's extraordinary work with leaders across the globe is legendary and reinforces the power that listening has in leadership effectiveness.

I am so thankful to my Leadership Mastermind Alliance members who gave me straight feedback after reading one of the many drafts. Their perspectives enabled me to re-direct the work into a more compelling creation. Thank you Armando Payas, Pat McLeod, Denise Messineo, Becky Nickol, Carl Chauncey, Ann Newhouse, Karen Randall, and Melinda Brody. I am also grateful to organizational consultant and coach Gearoid Hardy and Sales Executive Melody Giacomino who gave me very practical 'real world' recommendations.

I have been blessed by the editorial expertise of J.B. Adams, instructional designer and consultant, whose creative talents and writing were exceptional as he instilled practicality into the story. Additionally, I appreciate the diligent work of writer Rusty Fisher who transformed my ideas for a story line into a compelling fable.

My heartfelt appreciation goes to the James "Jay" Monroe for his superb design work of the book.

Above all, I am so grateful to my wife and best friend, Quin, who encouraged me throughout this entire project and offered me wise counsel when I needed it the most.

Prologue

Stu looked out into a sea of faces. Even though everyone was applauding, he sensed a mix of emotions in the room. Certainly, there were some who were shocked to hear his name; even Stu was a bit surprised. And there had to be a few who were disappointed to not hear their own names called. As Stu scanned the crowd, his eyes landed on an enthusiastic bunch in the corner—his team. It was their support that meant the most to him. He saw that Brad and Charlie were pumping their fists into the air. Rachel was beaming as she waved to him. And there was Linda, his assistant, jumping up and down and letting out a whoop.

The audience was still clapping as Stu moved across the stage, accepting congratulations from a line of company leaders. The trophy was heavier than he expected it to be, and he needed both hands to carry it. When he had a free moment, he looked down to examine his award. Etched into the crystal was the DynaCorp logo. Below were inscribed his name and the words *Sales Director of the Year.*

Stu was still taking it all in when his thoughts were interrupted. His boss, Carl Madison, tapped him on the shoulder.

"Stu, you did it!" Carl flashed a wide grin.

Stu nodded and returned the smile. He had to shift his grip on the trophy to shake Carl's hand.

"I have to tell you," Carl said, "coming from where you started, I wasn't sure you'd be standing here today."

Stu had been thinking the same thing. It had been only ten months since Carl had threatened to fire him.

"I'm honored . . . and humbled." Stu took a breath. In spite of all the attention, he was feeling a sense of serenity in the moment that he wanted to savor. "You'd probably never guess this, but that day in your office when you called me on the carpet was the first day of my new life."

"Oh, come on, now," Carl squawked. "You're giving me way too much credit."

Carl led Stu backstage as the next award was announced, and another ovation swept over the crowd. Stu waited for the applause to recede, then he turned to Carl. "I can't thank you enough. You gave me a wakeup call I will never forget."

Carl leaned in. "I'm proud of you!" he said, giving Stu a hug with one powerful arm.

As they entered the hallway, Carl turned to go back into the ballroom, until he noticed that Stu was no longer beside him. He spun around to see Stu, still standing in the doorway.

"Aren't you coming to the dinner?" Carl asked.

"You give them my regards," Stu replied.

Carl's eyes widened. "What?"

The annual sales conference was a very social event—the one time of the year when DynaCorp salespeople could catch up with old colleagues and make new contacts. Stu knew that as an award recipient, they would be expecting him to stay for the usual schmoozing and glad-handing. But he had other plans.

Carl's face relaxed into a smirk. "Part of the fun of winning the award is sticking around to let everyone congratulate you!"

"I'd love to, Carl," Stu smiled over his shoulder as he headed toward the exit. "But I've got somewhere I need to be!"

Carl sighed in acknowledgement, remembering that Stu had a special event of his own to attend. "I'll cover for you," he said, giving Stu a thumbs-up. "Good luck!"

● ● ●

Forty-five minutes later, Stu arrived at home, carrying a thoroughly prepared dinner he had picked up from the neighborhood's best caterer.

He found his wife, Jennifer, in the living room sipping a glass of wine. He reached out his hand; she stood and they warmly embraced.

Stu looked lovingly into his wife's eyes. "Happy third anniversary, babe," he whispered.

Jennifer glanced over at a large vase of flowers on the coffee table—a dozen roses that Stu had sent to her earlier in the day. "Thank you for the flowers, honey. They're so beautiful!"

"Not as beautiful as you," he grinned. "Stay here for a minute, I'll be right back."

Stu excused himself to turn on some soft music and light the candles in the dining room. He prepared two table settings—using the good dishes and silverware that were saved for special occasions—complete with a pair of white cloth napkins. Then he transferred the food to covered serving bowls; enticing aromas filled the house.

When everything was ready, Stu returned to the living room. He took Jennifer tenderly by the hand, picked up her glass of wine, and led her to the table.

As she entered the dining room, her eyes filled with emotion. There in the candlelight, she saw her favorite foods prepared for two. Stu pulled out her chair and gently slid it beneath her. Jennifer sat quietly, staring at the feast. It was clear to her that Stu had planned the details at least a month in advance.

"I can't believe you remembered how I said that for this anniversary, I just wanted a quiet night at home. You thought of everything. I mean, right down to my dream menu!"

Stu nodded. He wasn't ready to talk yet; emotion gripped his throat.

Jennifer continued. "It's quite a difference from last year's anniversary, remember?"

He shook his head and croaked, "How could I forget?"

Jennifer wasn't kidding, and Stu knew it. So much had changed in the past twelve months, it felt like a lifetime had passed. A year ago, he and Jennifer had been stuck in a pattern of misunderstandings, accusations, and hurt feelings. The tension came to a head around the time of their second anniversary, when Stu forgot the date and absent-mindedly planned an out-of-town business trip. For other couples, it might have been no big deal. But for Jennifer, this was the next to the last straw. She was furious with him, and the pain of that incident was so deep he wasn't sure they would recover.

After that, he vowed to Jennifer—and to himself—that this year would be different. It turned out that many things were different this year from last.

As if reading his mind, Jennifer raised her glass and said, "I'd like to make a toast!"

Stu smiled in anticipation.

"Even though it's *our* third anniversary, I want to recognize someone else for making tonight so very special," she said. "I want to thank Alfred D'Amato, for all he's done for you, for me, and for us. Without Alfred's wisdom and guidance, I hate to think where we were headed!"

Stu blushed and raised his glass to hers. "I couldn't agree more."

As the evening continued, they laughed, drank, and dined; it was a wonderful and memorable anniversary.

Later, Stu couldn't get Jennifer's words out of his mind: "Without Alfred's wisdom and guidance, I hate to think of where we were headed!"

She didn't have to finish the thought. Stu knew that without Alfred's counsel, he was less than a year away from another divorce. The things Stu learned from Alfred D'Amato had not only helped repair a troubled marriage; they also led to the improvements in Stu's performance at work. The day he met Alfred was the day Stu's life started turning around.

CHAPTER 1
The Writing on the Wall

If someone had told Stu Preston that this day would be a turning point in his life, he would have dismissed them for wasting his time. But a moment later, he would have thought: *Maybe I'm due for a change.*

For Stu, the day had started much like any other. He got up, ate a quick breakfast, responded to emails, checked his stock prices, and kissed his wife Jennifer on the cheek as she left for work. On his morning commute, he participated in a mobile phone conference call with the marketing department about the positioning of upcoming products. At 8:40 a.m. he arrived at the office.

As soon as he came in the door, his assistant reminded him that he had a ten o'clock meeting with three of his field managers. Linda always did her best to keep Stu in line. "You know it takes over an hour to get there, and you can't predict the traffic. I'll let them know you're on your way!"

He was in no hurry to attend the quarterly field meeting. In the past year, he had come to dread them.

Stu had worked at DynaCorp Plastics for twelve years, almost his entire career. When he was first hired as an entry-level sales representative, he said to himself: *What do I know about plastics?* He took the job to get some experience, and he did not intend to stay more than two years before moving on to greener pastures. Much to his surprise, he enjoyed selling plastics and came to embrace the company as well.

His rise through the ranks had been steady. He spent six years as a sales rep in various territories. Each time Stu moved to a new territory, he conquered it with an ease that got him noticed in the head office. Whenever they offered him a new territory, he was asked if relocating was a problem. His answer was always the same: *Take me to the challenge.* Never mind that moving around the country put additional strain on his marriage to his first wife, Deborah. Perhaps landing huge contracts and winning new clients helped divert Stu's attention from his problems at home. The reasons didn't matter; Stu loved his work and it showed. It was his attitude—and the associated results—that eventually led him to his place in DynaCorp management.

When he was promoted to sales manager of the Wallsey branch, he started reporting to Carl Madison. Stu immediately felt a kinship to Carl; they were both driven and ambitious. Carl was equally impressed by Stu's talent for sales. The longer they worked together, the more their mutual admiration grew.

Stu would never forget the moment he and Carl made their "success pact." Stu's sales team had just won a particularly valuable contract with the Leigh Brothers, a client Carl had pursued for years. At a sports bar around the corner from Carl's office, they shared a drink to celebrate "reeling in the big fish." Carl thanked Stu, expressed his satisfaction, and rhetorically asked, "How can I ever repay you?" Stu responded with a genuine request that was also a promise: *"I make you look good, you make me look good."* From that moment on, the two men operated with a devotion that was quietly reciprocated.

That commitment came to fruition two years later, when Carl was promoted to vice president of sales. There was much speculation about who would fill the open sales director job; certainly there were a number of qualified candidates. But no one at DynaCorp was surprised when Stu was selected to fill Carl's shoes.

Stu was proud to take on the responsibilities of sales director, and anxious for a new challenge. He was a little sensitive to the fact that, only in his early thirties, he was younger than most of the other sales directors. And it wasn't until he moved into the role that he became fully aware of the political hazards that plagued upper management.

When he interviewed for the position, he noted that it would be "cool" to continue working with his peers, since they all got along so well. It was only after he was in the role that he found out that his fellow sales managers, Rachel Gaines and Charlie Hartman—who both had more seniority than him—had also applied.

Once Rachel and Charlie became his direct reports, Stu immediately saw them change. On the surface, everything was fine, and they continued to get work done. But he could tell that something was lost; they didn't enjoy each other's company anymore. Their meetings had an underlying tension. Rather than address it up front, Stu chose to keep his team focused on the task at hand. He reasoned: *Why make matters worse by calling out their jealousy? They'll get over it soon enough.*

Stu's perception turned out to be right. In a few months, the tension subsided, and a new rapport was established. They brought some new faces onto the team, and work settled into a comfortable routine.

But after more than a year on the job, sales in his region started to slip. Over the following nine months, they continued to slide. It wasn't as if Stu could blame his poor numbers on a weak economy or a shift in the industry—sales directors in other regions were posting record numbers. Stu started to wonder if he was losing his touch. In a moment he later regretted, he mentioned his concerns to Carl. The response was swift: "You're the guy who used to say, 'Take me to the challenge.' Are you backing down from this one?"

The pressure of weak sales caused Stu to openly question his team and their abilities. He thought turning up the heat might help them raise their performance. Instead, the dynamic shifted back to the old tension and awkwardness. And over time, it turned into outright hostility.

It was 9:48 a.m. when Stu arrived at the rented conference facility for the quarterly sales managers' field meeting. He looked around the parking lot and saw three cars he recognized, indicating that his direct reports were already inside. For five minutes, he sorted his files and checked his phone for messages. For another five minutes, he idly watched a group of elementary school kids playing in a playground across the street. At 9:59, he got out of the car and slung his laptop bag over his shoulder. Looking up at the conference building with dismay, he muttered cynically to himself: *Take me to the challenge.*

• • •

"Have you even checked out the new reporting software, Stu?" Rachel's voice took on an accusing tone. Her face was pinched and sallow under the conference room's harsh fluorescent lights. "It's so overcomplicated . . . it's awful! I mean, it took me a full twelve minutes just to input a simple process—"

"Rachel," Stu interrupted, "I believe you mentioned that last month, when I asked you why sales at the Wycliffe branch might be off its monthly quota." Stu strained to keep the sarcasm out of his voice.

Rachel huffed, slipping a lock of her long black hair behind one ear. "I'm going to *keep* mentioning it until corporate *does* something about it. I won't have my sales performance unjustly knocked when it's a software issue that's underreporting our numbers. It's just wrong!"

"I've put in a complaint with Carl."

Stu was bluffing, but he had to do something to calm Rachel down. He rationalized that he was coming from a place of good intentions. Then, as soon as he said it, he realized he had meant to file a complaint with Carl . . . but had never gotten around to it.

"He's assured me he's doing everything in his power to alert corporate about the—"

"You said that last month," Rachel countered, drawing knowing smirks from the other two sales managers, Brad Chappelle and Charlie Hartman.

"What's so funny?" Stu snapped. He was eager for any diversion at this point; the argument over whether or not the new software was at the root of Rachel's low numbers had gone on for the last ten minutes. "It's not like you two are performing any better in *your* branches."

Charlie Hartman was sales manager of the Clark branch of DynaCorp. In Stu's mind, Charlie represented everything stereotypical about "old school" salesmanship. Weighing in at more than three hundred pounds, he was equal parts fat and muscle packed solidly into a six-foot-four-inch frame. Although Charlie was in his late fifties, he still wore the same trademark navy blazer and pleated khaki pants he'd always worn.

Meanwhile, Brad, who filled Stu's position as sales manager at DynaCorp's Wallsey branch, was at the other end of the spectrum. Only a few years out of college, he was dynamic, aggressive, ambitious—the kind of hot shot who was eager to let the world know about his every success. Unfortunately for Brad, he didn't have too many recent successes to brag about.

"Brad," Stu asked, zeroing in on him, "any explanation why *your* numbers slipped again this past month?"

Brad ran a manicured finger through his thick hair, avoiding Stu's eyes. "Like I told you, I've still got two open positions and I don't have enough talent on my team to keep up. Until I get some new blood, numbers are going to be weak. I feel like I'm working with a bunch of dinosaurs." Brad shot a glance over at Charlie and murmured, "No offense."

Before Charlie could realize he was being insulted, Stu remarked, "Charlie, your numbers were flat, but I guess that's better than going down."

"They would be better," Charlie insisted in his booming salesman's voice, "if the company would be a little more competitive with their pricing. My guys are gettin' killed at the bargaining table, Stu. What are you gonna do about *that*?" Charlie's face was turning a deep red.

Stu sighed. He knew as well as Charlie that the mandate from corporate was clear. Prices wouldn't go down until production sped up. And production wouldn't speed up until orders increased, and orders wouldn't increase until sales picked up. But he didn't feel like bringing it up again. *My hands are tied; it's a vicious circle I've explained a hundred times before.*

Stu held his hand up to his forehead and sighed again. He was tired of going round and round. Each of his sales managers had a favorite excuse. For Rachel, it was all about the software glitches. For Charlie, it was a constant war with pricing. For Brad, it was the "dinosaurs" on his sales team. They were always blaming someone else, never themselves, for their shortcomings. *Those kids on the school playground would be easier to manage than this bunch.*

"Listen," Stu said, eyeing the clock on the wall and reaching for his laptop case. "I know that DynaCorp isn't perfect, that the software has glitches, that pricing is a little higher than the competition, that our sales teams have more veterans than rookies . . . "

Stu noticed that each of his sales managers shifted and glanced nervously in response to hearing his or her own complaint.

"But you know what, guys? Deal with it! Rachel, you're lucky to have software to complain about. When I arrived here, the CRM software hadn't been updated in years. We had to fill out handwritten forms once a week—"

"That would be preferable to the system we have now," Rachel interjected coldly, crossing her arms over her chest. "At least then all of my sales would get registered and I wouldn't have to sit through an inquisition every month!"

Stu pursed his lips and nodded, as if he were paying attention. In reality, his rant was merely on pause. Only when Rachel stopped glaring at him did he turn to address Charlie and Brad.

"My point is, it's all about taking personal responsibility for you and your sales teams. You guys are my sales managers; I've got three of the best branches in the region, but back at headquarters they talk about us like we're a joke. You think I *like* comin' here once a quarter to badger you? Frankly, it's a pain in my butt. I have a thousand other things I could be doing back in my office instead of driving seventy-two miles to listen to your lame excuses."

Charlie opened his mouth to speak, but Stu gave him a look that cut him off. "I don't want to hear it!" Stu deliberately stared down each of his sales managers. "Not from any of you!"

"It's time to put up or shut up. I expect to see numbers up by next month. No more complaints, and no more excuses—or some of you might not have a very long future at DynaCorp."

Stu signified the meeting was over by shutting down and unplugging his laptop.

Charlie stood quietly, mumbled a farewell, and made a quick exit.

As Brad left, he looked pointedly at Stu with his mouth half-open, then thought better of it, smiled, and said, "Until next time."

Rachel lingered over her own laptop case, clicking pens and sliding in legal pads while Stu made himself look busy. Stu knew that Rachel wanted more one-on-one time with him; it was one of her many running complaints. But today Stu had two more stops to make before going back to his office, and he wasn't in the mood for another "what ails DynaCorp" lecture from her.

Rachel waited until Stu had zipped up his bag. Then, in a tone more level than she'd used during the one-hour meeting, she started, "Stu, if I could just—"

"Sorry, I've got to take a restroom break, and then I'm off to my next appointment," he insisted. He moved to hold the door for her as they walked into the hallway. "But if you can just give me five minutes, we can walk to my car and talk on the way . . . "

He let his voice trail off as he hustled through the men's room door, not waiting for a response. He knew by the time he came out of the restroom—hands double-washed, hair combed, and face washed with a wet paper towel or two—Rachel would have given up.

When he emerged from the restroom ten minutes later, he wasn't surprised to see that Rachel was gone.

CHAPTER 2
The Ultimatum

Stu raced in from the parking garage, laptop bag digging painfully into his right hip after stomping up four flights of stairs.

Linda, his executive assistant, was working over a stack of files. She looked up as he entered. "What'd you do now?" she asked.

"What?" Stu barked. "Like it's my fault the garage elevator isn't working again?"

"I wasn't talking about the elevator," Linda replied, furrowing her brow.

Linda Raleigh was in her middle years, petite with short hair and engaging brown eyes that she often hid behind dark-rimmed reading glasses. She had been Stu's assistant for the past two years, ever since his promotion. As a DynaCorp employee of more than twenty years, she was proud to say that she had seen the company through many changes.

Stu shuffled to his office; Linda stood and matched him step for step.

"Then what *are* you talking about?" Stu asked as he took his laptop bag off his shoulder and set it on his desk.

"Carl," she said. Her eyes widened as she glanced over the top of her glasses. "He said he wanted to see you the minute you got in."

Stu's heart was already racing from his hike up the stairs. Now he could feel it beating in his chest.

"Damn it," he whispered, just loud enough for Linda to hear him. "What does he want?"

"He didn't say. All I know is that he's waiting for you." She lingered near the doorway, her soft features now showing her concern.

Stu scowled as he passed Linda on his way out.

"Good luck!" she called after him half-heartedly. She sighed and went back to her filing.

• • •

Stu's pulse was still pounding when he knocked on Carl's half-open office door. A voice curtly replied, "Come in here!"

Carl Madison was DynaCorp's vice president of sales and Stu's direct superior. Carl had been with the company almost from its inception. Hired as an entry-level salesperson, he had patiently maneuvered his way up the ranks. He had more salt than pepper in his hair and more steel than honey in his baritone voice.

Stu entered to see Carl sitting at his neat and orderly desk. Carl was still looking at one of his three large computer monitors, checking the latest sales statistics from his many regional managers. Stu spent a moment lingering just inside the door.

When Carl failed to acknowledge him, Stu conspicuously cleared his throat. Then, softly, he asked, "You wanted to see me?"

Finally, Carl looked up, narrowing his gaze. Stu had seen this look before, and he knew that it didn't bode well for him.

"No," Carl said. "I didn't *want* to see you, Stu, but I *need* to see you. Please shut the door . . . and have a seat."

Stu stifled a groan. He knew that when Carl asked you to shut the door, you were in deep trouble.

Stu did as he was told, then slinked into the leather chair facing Carl's desk. Despite their long-standing relationship, he felt like a teenager who was about to be grounded.

Carl continued working at his computer keyboard while Stu's eyes scanned the room. Reminders of Carl's life dominated his office. There were framed newspaper clippings and trophies from Carl's days as a college football player; plaques and certificates praising Carl's superior salesmanship; and photos from Carl's family vacations, as he mugged for the camera with his wife and two daughters.

Finally Carl turned to face Stu. "What happened at your meeting today?" he muttered.

"What do you mean?"

"I mean that my phone has been ringing since your meeting ended there." Carl leaned back in his chair and stared.

Stu fumed at the thought of being ratted out by someone on his own team. *With all of the trouble they've been giving me, I can only guess which one it was....*

He shook his head. "I can't imagine why. The meeting was business as usual, the same old complaints and excuses. Don't worry," Stu added as he put hands on the edge of his chair to push himself up; he was ready to exit Carl's office and escape further scrutiny. "I'll get them whipped into shape and ... "

Carl raised an open hand to cut Stu off mid-sentence. He spoke in a low tone as he asked, "Did you tell Rachel that you'd spoken to me about getting rid of some software glitches in the sales tracking system?"

Stu sat back down. Clearly, the meeting wasn't even close to being over.

"Well ... sure," Stu stammered. His mind whirled to find a suitable excuse. "But that was just to put her off for a while. She's been complaining about those glitches for the last two months, and I've been meaning to ... "

Carl raised his hand again. He shook his head and lowered his voice even further.

"If she's been complaining about them for *two months*, then why am I just learning about them *now*? Do you have any idea how embarrassing it is to get a call from a sales manager and not have a single clue as to what she's talking about? I don't appreciate getting blindsided, Stu; not in the least. How would you feel if you had a complaint go unresolved for two months? Rachel is one of our top performers. We can't afford to lose her!"

Stu shook his head, gritting his teeth and imagining the rant he would unleash on Rachel the minute he got back to his office. *It takes some nerve for a subordinate to go behind the back of her boss to tell something that was shared in confidence—*

Carl interrupted Stu's internal tirade. "And what's this I hear about Charlie going on record about—of all things—corporate pricing?"

"Charlie called you, too?" Stu sighed, clenching his hands and resisting the urge to pound his fists on the desk. "Seriously, they're a bunch of whiners down there. Listen, I'm going to—"

"You want me to *listen* to you?" Carl barked. "What are you going to do, Stu? You're going to 'set them straight?' You're going to 'get them in line?' You're going to 'pull out all the stops?' Those are just some of the many excuses you've given me in the past few weeks. Six months this has been going on; *six months* I've been hearing rumblings from your sales managers with nothing to show for it except excuses."

Carl shook his head while Stu stared at the floor.

"Brad Chappelle told me you'd promised him you'd do something about recruiting some new blood into his office," Carl went on, leaning forward. "Did you really agree to that?"

Stu's mind was racing. *Rachel, Charlie, and Brad had all called Carl. Not only that, they'd apparently done so on the way back from this morning's meeting. I've got a mutiny on my hands!*

"Carl, listen . . . " Stu began sputtering, but his boss was having none of it.

"No," Carl interrupted, leaning forward even more to get Stu's attention. "I think it's *your* turn to listen. As a matter of fact, I think that's the whole problem: *you don't listen*. Not to me, not to your team, not to your clients. I simply *can't* be getting calls from your people, telling me you're threatening their jobs . . . telling me you're lying to them . . . telling me you're speaking on my behalf, without my permission. *I can't have that."*

Carl leaned back, sighing heavily.

"So what now?" Stu asked.

Carl took a deep breath to collect his thoughts, then continued deliberately. "I don't like having to do this, but I feel I have no choice . . . I'll give you six months. If you can't shape up . . . "

"Carl, there's no reason to go overboard. We can work this out . . . "

Carl raised his hand yet again. "Stu . . . please don't interrupt." He waited a second to make sure he had Stu's full attention.

"I've made up my mind . . . I'm giving you an ultimatum. If you can't reverse the downward direction of your performance, I'll have no choice but to terminate your employment with DynaCorp. You have six months."

Stu looked up, wide eyed and open mouthed. Carl met his gaze directly and waited patiently.

"An ultimatum...?" Stu's mind was racing. *I've known this man for years...we've helped each other succeed...and this is how he repays me...?*

"Is...this really necessary?" Stu rasped.

"It's for the best."

"But...I thought we had an agreement ..."

"An agreement?" Carl asked evenly.

"Yes," Stu bellowed. "Ever since we landed the Leigh Brothers account. Remember? *I make you look good, you make me look good.*"

"I remember," Carl said. "We did make a pact, and I've honored it."

"You honor it...," Stu muttered, "by giving me an ultimatum...?" He couldn't hide the emotion edging through his voice.

"I would continue to honor the pact," Carl explained, *"but you're not making me look good anymore."*

Carl's words cut deep. Stu took a labored breath and held his hand up to his forehead. There was a lingering moment of awkward silence.

Carl continued. "You know that this isn't personal. I think you're talented. But I can't ignore the facts. We've been seeing a drop in your sales over the past year and that trend hasn't turned around. The complaints from your people keep coming, and now they're getting louder. That doesn't make either one of us look good, and something has got to change. I'm giving you six months to fix it."

Stu blankly stood on stiff legs and inched toward the door. He felt like he was moving on autopilot as his stomach filled with leaden despair. He grasped the door handle, and turned to face Carl. His voice strained with emotion, Stu managed to squeak out, "Anything specific you're looking for in my performance?"

Carl paused, then carefully replied. "Yes, actually, there is. You need to listen better. Every one of those calls to my office today could have been avoided if you would really *listen* to what your people are telling you."

"No," Stu said, insistently. "I mean, anything *specific* I can do to improve my performance?"

Carl looked up at him, bemused. "Stu, this is *exactly* what I'm talking about! *You don't listen.* Not even to me! I just told you everything you needed to know to succeed, and you still didn't get it." He let out a heavy sigh. "Now if you'll excuse me, I need to make a phone call. Shut the door on your way out, will you?"

Stu nodded dejectedly as he left Carl's office, pulling the door closed behind him.

• • •

Stu shuffled back to his office in a state of shock, hardly noticing the midday activity that buzzed through the halls of DynaCorp headquarters. *What the hell just happened?*

He tried to sort out what could have caused three direct reports to be so disloyal. *Rachel and Charlie are still jealous that I got promoted ahead of them . . . and they still have strong relationships with Carl from the time when we all reported to him. But that doesn't explain Brad's betrayal and his boldness in circumventing me, going to Carl directly . . . maybe Rachel and Charlie are a bad influence on him. But then again . . .*

When he arrived back at his office, Linda was on the phone. He didn't even acknowledge her as he moved slowly through his doorway.

She quietly ended her phone conversation. "Stu just came in . . . I'll call you back later."

Stu closed his office door behind him. As he slid behind his cluttered desk, he gazed at a room holding commendations and awards for his years of service to the company. The plaques and certificates looked cold and foreign to him now.

Linda gave him just enough time to compose himself before she gently knocked on the door.

"Come in," Stu mumbled.

She slipped in gingerly, shutting the door and leaning up against it. "What happened with Carl?" she asked.

He looked up from his desk and shook his head. "I have no idea."

Linda frowned. "You must have some idea. Half the office saw you coming out of there."

Stu looked up; he hadn't considered how everyone in the office might interpret his dazed expression as he came out of the meeting. *I'll be the joke of DynaCorp—a twelve-year company veteran scolded like an unruly child.*

"Was it the Weston account?" Linda pressed. "I heard there were problems with that client."

"The Weston account?" Stu muttered. "No! Of course not." He paused. "Wait . . . what?"

He turned to look at Linda. Her comment about problems with Weston caught him off guard.

She gave him a blank stare.

"No, it was three brilliant sales managers," he said in a cynical tone. "Apparently they found enough brain power between them to all call Carl on the same day."

"What about?" Linda inquired. She had not moved from her protected perch near the doorway.

Stu waved a hand dismissively. "Does it even matter? The fact is, they've convinced Carl I'm—get this!—'a terrible listener.' Can you believe that?"

She looked down at her shoes, avoiding his gaze.

"Linda . . . ? What is it?"

"Oh, nothing," she said, looking up as if she'd suddenly been startled. "It's just that, you know . . . people have mentioned that before . . . about you not listening."

"What?" Stu exploded. He lowered his voice. "Who?"

Linda grimaced and held her hand up to her mouth, chewing on her fingernail as she formulated her response. "Uh . . . people around the office . . . they talk."

Stu squinted at her, frowning. "And what do 'they' say?"

She glanced around nervously. "Well, this shouldn't come as news, but . . . you've kind of earned a reputation for . . . being a little set in your ways . . . and, um . . . only hearing what you want to hear . . . "

She looked up to see that Stu was still squinting.

"Hmph," he scoffed. "So that's how the office assistant network spends their free time? Gossiping about my behavior?"

"Oh, it's not just *you* ... " Linda volunteered. "We talk about all the executives like that!"

"I see," Stu nodded. "Thanks, that makes me feel much better." he added sarcastically.

She tossed up her hands and shrugged.

"Wait a minute," he said. "Do *you* talk to them ... about *me*?"

"No, Stu," she replied quickly. "You know I have no complaints." She stared at him intently, as if she could convey her loyalty through mere eye contact.

After everything he had experienced in the past five hours, he could not bear the thought of Linda not being on his side. *I have to trust her ... she takes good care of me and she has no reason to lie. Besides that, she might be the only one I have left.*

"But," Linda added, "um ... I think you need to know ... "

Stu raised his eyebrows in anticipation.

"That reputation isn't based on what the office assistants think," she said. "It's what some of the other VPs and sales directors mention to their assistants ... that's what gets relayed back to me."

Stu took a breath and tried to process all he was hearing. *Can I rely on second-hand information? Should I even care about what they think?*

Stu grumbled."Well, even so ... those three had no business ganging up on me like that. And if they think I'll forget about it, and that their problems will go away because Carl chewed me out, they've got another thing coming."

"I dunno," said Linda, biting her lower lip. "I mean . . . they had to have been pretty upset in order to call Carl. Maybe you should just lay low for a while, and do what he says . . . "

"Do what he says? What he says . . . is that I have six months . . . to shape up or ship out."

Linda's eyes widened. "Really?" she asked.

"Basically, yeah. He said if I don't get my numbers up, and he doesn't hear glowing reports from those misfits before my next six-month review, I'm outta here. How's that for a mutiny? Those three are in for a rude awakening. I'll come down on them so hard they won't know what hit them ..."

Stu looked up to see that Linda was frowning. He knew what that meant: once again, he had gone too far, saying things out loud that should have stayed in his head.

Before she could school him on controlling his tongue, Stu abruptly stood and announced, "Sorry . . . I'm heading home for the day. I need to collect my thoughts."

Linda looked ruffled as Stu reached for his laptop bag and brushed by her. Soon, however, her expression changed to one of acceptance. "Good idea," she said simply as she returned to her own desk. "Take some time, think it all over. Tomorrow will be a better day . . . "

Stu, unconvinced, absently nodded his goodbye.

Still shaken and cranky over Carl's ultimatum, Stu approached the parking garage elevator. A handwritten "out of order" sign had been hastily taped over the call buttons, indicating that he would be walking down four flights of stairs.

As he entered level two of the garage, a cool mist hit his face. He turned to look out over the tops of the parked cars, and saw thick gray clouds churning across the sky. *Bad weather on its way . . . maybe I can get home before it hits.*

A loud crack of thunder told him that he was too late.

CHAPTER 3
Close Call

As Stu walked through the parking garage, he heard the random tapping of a few huge rain drops; by the time he located his black Porsche, it had become a steady downpour.

The foul weather further dampened Stu's mood. *It doesn't matter that I'm leaving the office early . . . a heavy rain like this means slow traffic all the way home. Could this day get any worse?*

With his wipers whipping back and forth, he set out into the deluge. The air was so humid that a layer of condensation formed on the windshield, hindering his view. He turned on the defogger to try and clear his vision, but the dampness was too thick—a steamy ring persisted around the edge of the window. *It doesn't matter; everyone out here is moving at a crawl.*

Not in any mood to turn on the radio, he sat silently, carefully watching the brake lights of the cars in front of him. Between the sluggish traffic, the reduced visibility, and the steady clatter of the rain, Stu felt like he was wrapped up inside a cocoon—isolated, but not comfortable.

He pondered his options.

Leave DynaCorp? The thought hadn't crossed his mind until today. He had been so satisfied with the company, the work, and his progress up the corporate ladder that he hadn't considered working anywhere else. And he hadn't kept up with any colleagues who had moved on to other companies, either. After all the time and effort he had invested at DynaCorp, finding a position at another company felt like starting over.

The alternative was to address the problem, face it head on. He had thought that being soft on his sales managers—trusting them to be professionals and hold themselves accountable—was enough to get them to perform. Obviously, the soft sell wasn't working. *Those malcontents need a wake-up call . . . and I'm just the guy to give it to them.*

Stu had known Carl Madison long enough to know that his boss didn't issue idle threats. But the assertion that Stu's performance would improve if he just listened better sounded completely ridiculous. *Carl's got it all wrong. It doesn't have anything to do with poor listening . . . it's all because of the misguided motivations of some incompetent managers.*

However, upon reflection, Stu had to acknowledge that Carl was right about one thing. *I guess I have been working at half-capacity for the last six months or so . . . maybe longer if I cared to admit it.*

His angry reverie continued until he finally saw the entrance to his subdivision in the distance. Stu checked his dashboard clock; a commute that usually took twenty minutes had taken a full hour. The rain was still hammering down, and the streets were starting to look more like canals.

Instead of calming his nerves, the time spent thinking had only gotten him more agitated. It didn't help that his car was jammed up with hundreds of other vehicles on a four-lane boulevard, merely creeping along while his destination was in plain sight.

When the opportunity presented itself, Stu cut off another driver and nudged over so he could get into the right lane. About two hundred yards from the turn-off, he cranked the steering wheel and started driving on the edge of the road, bypassing traffic on the right-hand side. As he turned to enter his neighborhood, he breathed a sigh and gunned the engine a bit. *The way home is clear! Finally . . . some relief from all this waiting!*

As he turned onto his street, he remembered the cryptic statement that Carl had made: *"You need to listen better."* Yet even when pressed, his boss couldn't explain specifically what he wanted. *That's okay . . . it probably just means I need to be nicer to people . . . more patient.*

Stu decided that the long drive had helped him sort out his thoughts, and he knew how to move forward. Even though he was still angry about the whole affair, he saw that he was due for a change, and this was an opportunity to grow. *I'm going to double-down on making things work. Carl wants results? He'll get them. Nothing is going to get in my way.*

Suddenly, Stu gasped. A flashing red light had jumped into his field of vision, and he slammed on his brakes. A wave of muddy water sprayed up onto his windshield.

Using his index finger, he wiped away the dew on the window to get a clearer view. Just a few feet in front of him, a large van had stopped in the middle of the road.

"Get out of the way, idiot!" Stu cursed.

Then he noticed that the van's hazard lights were blinking. Regaining his bearings, Stu saw that he was only about five doors away from his house.

Pulling his car ahead, he sidled up to the van. There was no driver to be seen, but it was still too dark and rainy to tell for sure.

Disgusted and anxious to be home, Stu pushed on the gas again. As he bounded into his own driveway, another obstacle leapt out in front of him.

Stu saw the downed oak tree just in time to swerve out of the way. But in doing so, he smashed through another mud puddle and skidded into the flower bed that ran parallel to the driveway.

He stopped for a moment, rolled down his window, and saw that a large tree branch was blocking his way— but there was just enough space to get around it to reach his garage. He tapped the gas pedal, but the car just rocked a bit as the wheels sputtered and spun in the mire. Chunks of dirt and grass knocked against the fenders.

After all the drama of the day, Stu was at his wit's end. *I've had it!*

Enraged, he slammed on the gas. The wheels buzzed and rolled as the back end of the car shimmied out to the left, flinging mud in all directions and cutting a deep gash across his water-soaked lawn. A few seconds later, the car found enough traction to jerk back up onto the driveway.

Stu's heart was pounding as he pulled into the garage. He slammed the car door and staggered into the house, going straight to the refrigerator to crack open a beer.

About an hour later, Jennifer arrived at home.

"Stu, what happened out here?" she called as soon as she got in the door. "Stu?"

Stu didn't answer.

"The front yard is a mess!" she yelled. She found him in the living room, reclined on the couch, watching TV. "Is everything okay?" she asked in a troubled tone of voice.

"It's fine," Stu said, without averting his eyes from the television.

"Care to explain what happened out there?" she asked, clearly irritated.

"I'll take care of it this weekend," he said.

"That's your explanation?"

Stu did not respond.

She sighed and folded her arms, noticing the three beer cans and half-eaten microwave pizza on the coffee table in front of him. "I think I'm gonna go meet Caroline for dinner . . . ," she said.

"Great," he replied blankly.

Jennifer quietly left the house.

Stu sighed, relieved that his wife did not question him any further. *Thank God she let it go . . . I could not handle one more confrontation today.*

• • •

As Stu sat on the couch, he pondered the events of the day.

While he wasn't surprised by Jennifer's withdrawal, he was somewhat taken with how quickly it had happened. *She doesn't usually give up that easily.*

Things hadn't been going well in the Preston household for several months. He couldn't quite put his finger on the problem; he surmised that he had probably been spending too much time on work, and not paying enough attention to her. *Maybe I'm overdue for getting her a nice piece of jewelry.*

But Jennifer was not the type to be swayed by an expensive gift.

Stu loved and appreciated his wife, even though he had trouble telling her so. *She knows I love her, because of the things I do . . . I don't have to say it.*

In considering what he loved most about her, he couldn't help but compare Jennifer to his first wife, Deborah.

Stu met Deborah in college, when they sat next to each other in a business class. She was lively and flirtatious, and she fueled his ego.

Their romance made them popular on campus, and they got engaged before graduation. They continued their engagement for several years without setting a wedding date. The decision was mutual; as they often mentioned to inquiring family members, they were both "focused on starting careers." When they finally did get married, it seemed like the right thing to do, as they socialized with a group of upwardly mobile couples.

Deborah shared Stu's interest in achievement and competition. It was this passion to win that made her attractive to Stu from the beginning. He remembered fondly the times they would be jogging in the park, challenging each other to race. They couldn't play a simple video game without a teasing one-upsmanship. Over time, this trait became the downfall of their relationship. When a disagreement occurred, neither could back down; there was too much pride at stake. If one of them proved the other wrong, the other would be humiliated while the winner earned the right to gloat. When they were first starting out, each little spat always led to a passionate making up. Over time, the spats changed into shouting matches, and the make-ups generated less and less passion. They were married for about two years before things turned sour. An entire year was spent in an ongoing cycle of distrust and bickering. Another three years brought half-hearted reconciliations and counseling attempts. And then they called it quits.

Stu thought he would enjoy being single again, but instead he found it rather lonely. It was a few months after finalizing the divorce that he met Jennifer at a dinner party. He was intrigued by her; she was so different from Deborah. Jennifer was quiet and thoughtful in a way that made her mysterious. She was beautiful, but she didn't need to be the center of attention. Still, he could see the passion in her whenever he would ask her about her work as a school teacher and she described her desire to make a difference in the lives of children.

On one of their first dates, Jennifer playfully accused Stu of using old sales techniques in order to charm her. They both shared a laugh, and he realized that he would have to raise his game if he was going to win her over. Compared to his previous relationship, their courtship did not last long; it was only nine months before he asked Jennifer to marry him, and the wedding was a mere three months later.

When he was with her, Stu noticed that he was able to slow down and enjoy life more. Even after they married, she insisted they keep up the practice of a weekly date on Sunday nights, to enjoy each other's company over dinner and a movie. Stu thought he had found his bliss in Jennifer.

But now, two years into their marriage, Stu could see that things weren't working between them—and he couldn't explain why. Jennifer didn't confront him the way that Deborah had. Where Deborah was determined to fight to the bitter end, Jennifer was more likely to cry, or to simply pull away.

Stu realized that his second marriage was starting to look like his first. He and Jennifer had fallen into a similar pattern of distrust and miscommunication. In retrospect, he could see that with Deborah, there had been no hope of patching things up; they were too much the same. But he didn't feel that way about Jennifer. Recognizing how good things had been with her—and how patient she could be—made him certain that they could figure things out. He wished he knew what the answer was. The lack of a clear path made the situation all the more confounding to him.

• • •

It was after ten o'clock when Jennifer returned. After entering the house, she quietly came into the living room, where Stu was still watching TV. Before he could speak, she said, "I'm going to bed. Good night." She walked down the hallway and closed the bedroom door softly behind her.

Stu went back to his thoughts. In the time she had been gone, he had watched a basketball game and tried to make sense of his life. He hadn't come to any major revelations. *These things weren't my fault, so why should I be the one who suffers? Even so ... I might be due for a change.*

CHAPTER 4
A New Day Dawns

The next morning, earlier than usual, Stu arose to begin his six-month "probation" at DynaCorp. Despite his lingering resentment to the entire situation—and just a bit of a hangover—he was determined to address the challenge set before him and show his boss Carl that he could, in fact, perform.

As the garage door rose, Stu peeked outside to examine the full extent of his battle with yesterday's storm. Tire tracks across the lawn still held puddles of dirty water. Jennifer's flower bed had been flattened. The front yard looked like the aftermath of county fair tractor pull.

More important to Stu, though, was the toll taken on his black Porsche; the auto was caked and spattered with crusty mud. Seeing the condition of his car brought back all the pain and frustration of the previous day. Nevertheless, there was no time for cleaning. Stu had decided to get his "new program" started by arriving to work by 7:30 am.

The early hour meant there was little traffic to fight with; Stu was able to make it to the office in record time. Yet, every few seconds, he was annoyed to hear the ding of small dirt clods knocking against his car, as the dried mud, bit by bit, fell from the fenders and wheel wells.

As he pulled into the DynaCorp parking facility, he recalled how yesterday's broken elevator had caused him to hike up four flights. Taking advantage of his good memory and the relatively empty garage, he decisively drove past vacant parking spaces to reach a higher level of the garage. *I'm on top of things today.*

He rounded the corner to see that level six was empty, but not as empty as he expected it to be. In a cluster near the stairway were several cars and one bright white van.

Curious to know what would attract people up to this parking level at such an early hour, Stu parked his car nearby, strapped on his laptop bag, and strolled past the cars toward the stairway entrance.

As he came close to the van, he realized that he wasn't alone. He could hear the soft sounds of scrubbing and the slow hiss of a hose. There was also the powerful scent of "clean." On the other side of the white van, he saw a brand-new Mercedes sedan, completely covered in frothy foam. Standing next to it was a fifty-something-year-old man dressed in white coveralls, applying the last bit of suds to the rear bumper.

Stu looked back at his Porsche, covered in grime, and realized a good auto detailing would be just the thing to help erase his unpleasant memories of the previous day. He approached the man from behind, clearing his throat to get his attention.

When that got no response, he called out, "Nice job!" Again, nothing.

Stu frowned. *Either this guy is hard of hearing or he's completely lost himself in his work.*

Only when Stu got a little closer did the man turn and notice him. With a surprised expression, the older gentleman smiled, showing a kind face that was weathered from years of working in the sun. His graying hair was cut short and tight, like he had served in the military.

The man put down his foaming gun and reached for something in the top pocket of his white coveralls. Quickly, his thick fingers plucked out a small, curved tool of some sort. He reached up to the side of his head; it took only a moment for him to slip on what was clearly a high-tech hearing device.

Accustomed to seeing the old-fashioned hearing aids that wrapped around the ear and plugged inside, Stu was amazed not only by the device's strange shape, but also the man's agility in inserting it.

"Hello," the gentleman said. "I'm Alfred D'Amato!" He spoke slowly, with the careful pronunciation of someone who had struggled with a lifetime of hearing loss. It was only then that Stu spotted the large circular logo on the side of the van: "D'Amato Detailing."

The older man extended a warm and slightly soapy hand.

Stu gave Alfred his best salesman's grip. "Stu Preston," he announced. "I was just admiring your work."

"Thank you," Alfred smiled again. "Are you interested in some detailing? I can make your car shine like new."

"Actually, I am," Stu said. He motioned over his shoulder toward his dirty Porsche.

"Oh," Alfred grunted slightly, obviously stunned by the sight. He walked briskly over to the car to take a closer look. Stu had no choice but to follow.

"This is from yesterday's rain?" Alfred inquired.

"Well, not all of it, but . . . anyway, I would love to have your help in getting rid of all this mud."

"What happened?" Alfred asked innocently.

"It's kind of a long story," Stu said.

Alfred shrugged and pointed toward the Porsche. "I've got a few minutes while this foam does its business. Why don't you tell me about it? I'm happy to listen."

Stu hesitated. He wasn't sure he wanted to talk about it, but after a moment he reconsidered. *It might be good to get it out of my system before I go into the office . . . and this guy seems trustworthy.*

"Well, I don't want to take up too much of your time, but . . . all this mud is like a nasty reminder of one really long, really awful day. I've been dealing with some difficult people at work . . . my boss gave me an ultimatum and told me I need to listen better . . . I have a tree blocking my driveway, I got stuck in the mud . . . and somebody drove through my front yard."

Alfred gave a quizzical look, but let Stu continue.

"So it would mean a lot to me to have a clean car again . . . kind of like a fresh start, if that makes any sense," Stu said. "Think you can help me out?"

Alfred grinned gently. "I can," he replied. "Maybe in more ways than expected."

"Uh . . . okay," Stu said. "Can you do it today?"

"Oh, sorry," Alfred said. "I'm fully booked today, but I'll be back here later this week, on Friday afternoon."

"Thanks, I'll take it." Stu took out his phone to make the appointment.

Alfred tilted his head curiously. "If I may, I'd like to go back to something else you mentioned."

Stu looked up from his phone, uncertain of what the old man meant.

"You said that your boss wanted you to listen better . . . is that right?" Alfred asked.

"Yes, that's right."

Alfred smiled confidently. "I can help you with that, too, if you like."

Stu scoffed a bit, then did his best to hide his amusement. "Oh, that's okay . . . I've got it under control," he smirked. "Thanks, just the car detailing will be fine."

"Very well," Alfred said, still smiling.

Stu went back to booking the appointment, trying not to roll his eyes. *What could a deaf man teach anyone about listening?*

Then he closed up his phone. "And how much do you charge?" he asked.

In a neutral tone, Alfred shared his price for a single detailing service. Shocked at the amount, Stu tried to maintain a poker face. *That's more than half of a monthly car payment!*

Before Stu could reply Alfred added, "But you look like an extreme case."

"What?" Stu shot back, hardly believing his ears.

Alfred winked slightly while adding, "Sorry, did I say *'you'* look like an extreme case? I meant *your car* looks like an extreme case. In any event, I'm running a special right now; services provided twice a month, six months for the price of five. You'll save—"

"Done!" Stu said, eager to lock in the savings before Alfred could rethink his offer. *The price is steep, but it's worth it . . . and it will be my reward for adopting a new attitude.*

"You'll have to sign a six-month commitment to hold that price," Alfred said warily.

"Sure, fine," Stu said, readjusting his laptop bag. "See you here on Friday?"

"See you then, Stu."

Alfred reached into another pocket on his spotless coveralls and pulled out a business card. Stu went to grab it but Alfred held on gently. Only when Stu looked up to make full eye contact did Alfred smile and say, "I look forward to our partnership."

"Thanks, I do too," Stu said. He turned to exit the parking garage. Before tucking the business card away, he glanced down at it. On it he saw the same circular logo and slogan that were painted on the side of the van: "D'Amato Detailing: Paying Attention to What Matters Most."

• • •

About an hour later, still early that morning, Stu's assistant Linda strode into the office. She was surprised to find the door already unlocked and the lights turned on. She poked her head into Stu's doorway. "What are you doing here?" she asked.

"I decided to come in early to review some paperwork," Stu said. "Ready for some coffee?"

"Okay . . . I'll get it started," she replied. She went back to her desk to set down her bag.

Stu got up from his chair, still carrying the files he was studying. He leaned against the doorway. "I already made some," he said. "It's sitting on your desk, just the way you like it. Two creams, one sugar, right?"

Linda's mouth was agape as she turned to look at him. It pleased him to think that she was genuinely surprised by his thoughtfulness.

Still wearing a quizzical look on her face, she picked up the cup and took a cautious sip. The scene made him smile; the coffee was still warm enough to fog up her glasses.

"Well," she said good-naturedly, "I actually take mine with two sugars and no cream, but ... this'll work!"

Stu's face dropped with disappointment. He had wanted to start the first day of his "new program" on the right foot—arriving early, going the extra step of brewing the first cup of coffee—and he'd gotten it wrong. *Maybe Carl was right; maybe I do need to do a better job of listening.*

Linda noticed his distress, and tried to soothe him. "Don't worry . . . it's just coffee. And it's the thought that counts, right?"

Stu gave her a weak smile.

"Whatcha lookin' at there?" she asked, referring to the thick folder he held in his hand.

Stu's face dissolved into an insecure frown. "My past two performance evaluations from Carl."

"Oh," she said carefully. "Finding any answers in there?"

He flipped open the file to glance through the pages. "I'm not sure," he replied. "After what Carl said yesterday, I kept thinking he had to be wrong. I wanted proof . . . proof of how wrong he was, you know? So I came in here early, and rummaged through the files until I found these."

Linda took another sip of her coffee. With a hopeful tone, she said, "Well, I know you and Carl have a good relationship, so . . . aren't they mostly good?"

He nodded hesitantly. "I guess they are . . . but I'm seeing some things in here I didn't notice before."

Linda turned her eyes away and took another drink.

Stu continued. "Carl's review meetings are usually pretty quick. He just says. 'Your numbers keep going up!' and then we talk about my direct reports. He always puts something in here about my development, but that's just because he has to."

He paged through the evaluation reports and realized he had an opportunity to make his point. *I've always trusted Linda's opinion, and she has never feared giving it to me.*

"I'd like to get your take on something," he said.

Linda opened her mouth to say something, but then stopped and took another drink of coffee instead. She moved to her chair to sit down, wearing an expression of guarded resignation.

"Listen to this comment from last year's review." He read aloud from the document. "'*Stu is an energetic self-starter who works well independently, but suffers in a challenging group dynamic. He doesn't handle confrontation well and often upsets those on his team. Improved listening would enhance his overall performance.*' Now . . . do you think that sounds like me?"

"The good parts do," Linda offered diplomatically.

Stu waited a moment. It appeared to him that she was holding something back. He goaded her. "But . . . ?"

"But *what*?" she smirked, shifting nervously in her seat.

"I hear a 'but' in there. Come on! I really need your help with this."

"Oh, in that case," she grinned, to soften the blow. "Well, I was just going to say that you *are* a little bit . . . *prickly* . . . with people . . . when you think they're wrong."

"Yeah, because . . . they're wrong!" he flared, feeling some heat rise to his face. "What good does it do to coddle people who can't keep up?"

Linda nodded, pursing her lips. "I see. But have you ever thought about it in a different way? Maybe it's not that they're 'wrong,' as much as they need a little help to see how you're 'right.'"

Stu frowned. "I have to *help* them? You mean I should *do their jobs* for them?"

Linda jumped in. "Okay, I can see that this is where your 'self-starter' personality comes in, but . . . Stu, not everyone is like you. Some people are more than qualified for the job, but they might also need a little help and support from above."

"That's nonsense," Stu spat. "Do you see me getting any support from above? Carl signs my paycheck, that's about it. Anything I've earned, I've gotten the hard way. It's kind of hypocritical for Carl to count my 'self-starter' personality against me when he's certainly never offered me a bit of help!"

Linda waited a beat before asking, "Have you ever *asked* him for help?"

Stu snarled in disgust. "No! Why would I? The boss hires you to *solve* problems, not *create* them. Look at us—you and me, you never ask me for help, and I don't punish you for it!"

Linda held up her hands in a "you win" gesture before continuing. "Okay, okay, I get that, but . . . I can tell you that I *would* expect your help if I ever had a problem I couldn't handle on my own."

Stu looked at her more closely. "So what are you saying? I'm too proud to ask for help?"

"I didn't say that. I said that it's okay for people to need help . . . and to ask for it. Bosses nowadays aren't just for signing checks."

"Well, yeah ... but I don't want to turn into one of those pathetic wimps who can't solve his own problems ... someone who's always knocking on the boss's door for every little issue."

"I agree," Linda said. "I just wonder ... is that the message you're sending to *your* direct reports?"

"Is *what* the message?" he asked.

"That you don't want them to be all clingy and needy; that you want them to solve their own problems."

"Exactly!" Stu said. *Finally, she is starting to get my point!*

"Okay, but ... if they get the message to never bother you with their problems, who do you think they'll go to when they're looking for help?"

"Who?" Stu asked. He took a thoughtful breath and studied Linda's face. "Carl?"

She nodded quietly.

"That's my point exactly," he said. "I work with a bunch of complainers who can't handle their own responsibilities."

Linda rolled her eyes discreetly, but Stu caught it nonetheless.

He frowned at her and read on.

"How about this one from two years ago? '*Stu continues to excel in an individual capacity, but his inability to focus on the issues at hand is starting to affect his ability to lead and influence others. In meetings, Stu has difficulty listening to diverse opinions that are different from his own.*' Does that sound like me?"

Linda paused and blinked. Then she turned away to fire up her computer, stating simply, "No comment!"

Stu frowned and closed the folder. *She is clearly siding with Carl.*

"Fine," he said. He went back into his office to grab his laptop bag and mobile phone from his desk. "We can talk more about this later on. I've got to get on the road or I'll be late."

"On the road?" she said, obviously shocked. "Wait; hold on. I thought you were in the office today."

"There has been a change in plans," he said confidently as he passed by her desk. "I've got a meeting with Rachel at the Wycliffe branch. It's at eleven o'clock and I don't want to be late."

"Today?" Linda asked. "But it's not the end of the month! And you never go all the way to the branches!"

"It's the new me," Stu called out as he headed for the stairs. "So get used to it!"

CHAPTER 5
Listening Is a Gift

On Friday afternoon, Stu sat in the employee cafeteria downstairs from his office, nursing a lemonade and listlessly pushing a chopped salad around in its bowl.

He wasn't really hungry, and he knew that eating so late would derail his appetite for the rest of the day, but he was killing time while his car finally got detailed. And, lately, sitting in his office was the last place he wanted to be.

He stared at his mobile phone, awaiting the signal from the old man at D'Amato Detailing to let him know that his car was ready. Around him, cafeteria workers were quietly shutting down for the day, cleaning out the steam tables and taking off their white aprons and hair nets. He tried to appreciate the serenity of the empty cafeteria, but his mind kept turning back to his recent meeting with Rachel, his sales manager at the Wycliffe branch.

Usually Stu and Rachel met halfway between head-quarters and her office—though according to Rachel, describing the arrangement as "halfway" wasn't accurate. She often complained about having to drive considerably farther than Stu did for the meetings. In Stu's mind, that was Rachel all over. *Nothing is ever good enough for her, and if there is a way to complain about something, she'll find it.*

Stu's usual response to her "not quite halfway" complaint was a simple one: *Rank has its privileges.*

At any rate, this particular meeting was intended to be different. Stu, putting effort into his "new program" and not wanting to add more grievances onto Rachel's list, saved her a trip and drove all the way out to her branch.

The meeting got off to a good start. As Stu entered Rachel's office, she greeted him with a friendly smile and handshake. However, the positive momentum didn't last long.

Stu thought she might genuinely appreciate that he had saved her a trip. But in her own mildly sarcastic tone, she said, "Wow, it's not often that you come *way out here.* To what do I owe this honor?"

Stu gritted his teeth against her fake smile and said, "You know why I'm here. When one of my regional managers complains to Carl, it's my policy to follow up on it personally."

"Since when?" Rachel huffed, rolling her eyes. "I've been talking about this for the past three or four months and this is the first response I'm getting from you *or* Carl."

Stu tried to contain his irritation, as he explained, "Well . . . in case you've forgotten . . . as director of sales for our region, I have a number of sales managers I have to supervise, and I can't be running off to every branch, every time one of them tattles on me."

He knew he had chosen the wrong word the moment it left his mouth.

"*Tattle?*" Rachel asked. Her voice grew higher and louder. "Is *that* what you think I did?"

"You tell me. I've always been open and honest with you. I don't understand why you didn't feel like you could talk to me first, before going over my head!"

Rachel quietly fumed, her face growing flush with emotion until she finally exclaimed, "What do you think I've been trying to do for the last three months? Every meeting, every month, I bring up the same issue and nothing ever gets done about it. It's like you're not even listening to me!"

Stu flinched. There was that word again: *listening*.

He thoughtlessly retorted, "Well, it's hard to take you seriously when you harp on the same thing over and over."

Again, Stu realized too late; it was a poor choice of words. Not surprisingly, the meeting went downhill after that. He made some attempts to get the conversation back on track, even bringing up other topics he knew were important to her. But he could tell there was no bringing her back. He spent the rest of the meeting reciting his standard talking points.

Stu was jolted out of his daydream when his phone signaled an incoming text message. He checked it and saw it was from Alfred at D'Amato Detailing: *Beauty awaits, sir.*

He trashed the rest of his midday meal and hustled up the stairs to the parking garage, too impatient to wait for the still unpredictable elevator. He emerged from the stairwell and turned the corner, startled to see his formerly dirty Porsche sparkling with a showroom-quality sheen.

"Amazing," said Stu. *The car doesn't just look new; it looks better than new!*

Alfred didn't notice Stu's presence. He remained hunched over a front wheel, putting the finishing touches on the glistening wire rims. Stu remembered that Alfred couldn't hear him, so he carefully walked around the car and into Alfred's line of vision.

Alfred looked up and smiled. Then he stood in his spotless white jumpsuit and pulled the blinking blue hearing device from his pocket and slipped it into his ear.

"What do you think?" Alfred asked with curiosity.

Stu was still in awe as he circled the car, seeing his reflection beaming back in everything from the windows to the outer casing of the rearview mirrors. "I'm blown away, really. I've never seen such attention to detail."

Alfred nodded, pleased to hear Stu's compliment. "Excellent! That's what we say D'Amato Detailing is all about: paying attention to what really matters!"

Stu cocked his head. "I've been meaning to ask you about that."

"Yes?"

"I worked in advertising for a bit after college. You have a unique slogan. What does it mean, exactly?"

Alfred smiled gently and said, "It's simple, really. I don't just *wash* your car and polish it up. Detailing work requires very careful attention. I like to think that I actually *listen* to your car while I'm working. Your car tells me what really matters. I go where it tells me to go, do what it needs the most. It really sets me apart from other detailers."

"Okay," Stu said, grinning as he patted Alfred playfully on the shoulder. "Seriously? *The car talks to you and you listen to it?* That's a good one, man," Stu sarcastically nodded and winked.

Alfred gave Stu a fretful look before continuing, "I hope I'm not misunderstanding you. Listening is no joke to me."

"Oh . . . of course," said Stu, backpedaling. "I'm sorry if I offended you." He nodded toward the device in Alfred's ear. "Yes, I've seen your hearing aid."

"It's more than a hearing aid," Alfred explained, his voice growing quiet and serious. "You see, when I was only three, I got a severe case of the German measles, and I lost my hearing as a result. It was sudden and over-night . . . a life-defining experience. I grew up deaf, and thought I'd always stay that way."

"Sorry to hear that," Stu murmured, unsure of the right words to say.

Alfred smiled and said, "Don't be sorry; I'm not."

"You're not?" asked Stu.

"No . . . not at all. You see, growing up deaf taught me how to listen with more than just my ears. I can read lips, and watch body language. I feel the vibrations around me; it's almost like I gained extra senses by growing up that way."

"But . . . you can hear now, right?"

"When I was forty-one years old, I received a cochlear implant, and for the first time in my life, I was able to *really* hear."

"Is that what that is?" Stu asked, pointing to Alfred's right ear.

"Yes," Alfred smiled proudly. "After only one medical procedure, this device helped me to hear for the first time since I was three!" His eyes were alive with appreciation. "It's so powerful, I call it my 'bionic ear.'"

Stu had to admit that he was impressed by Alfred's story. *Imagine, losing one of your senses for most of your life and then, bam, in one day, you get it back! What a powerful gift!*

"Wow," Stu commented. "Getting your hearing back must have been quite an adjustment."

"Yes, it was . . . such an adjustment, in fact, that I decided to go back to school to learn how to really listen."

The word "listen" hit Stu like a smack in the face, calling to mind Carl's ultimatum and Rachel's unfounded accusations.

"I attended evening classes at the college so it wouldn't interfere with my business," Alfred went on. "Really listening to the professors' lectures was thrilling for me. Hearing the discussions of my fellow students and actively participating in the educational debates was like getting a second chance in life. I was thrilled with the opportunity to listen and to communicate. I was so interested in learning about how these skills affect our lives, I decided to pursue a major in communication. I graduated with a degree in organizational communication at the age of forty-seven."

"Congratulations," Stu said, appropriately impressed.

"That's not the end—it gets better. One of the requirements in my studies was a course in listening."

"That's ... interesting," Stu interjected, intrigued by the coincidence in his circumstances. He shook his head. "You mean they actually offer a course on listening?"

"You bet," Alfred nodded simply. "And it changed my life. It was taught by a man who ultimately became my mentor. His name was Dr. Grover Sladaczewski—everybody called him 'Dr. Grove' for short, and he was an expert in the field of listening and leadership."

Stu blinked before asking, "So you were serious when you said you actually 'listened' to the cars?"

"Now you're getting it," Alfred remarked, gently smiling. "When I work on a car, I take off my implant and set it aside."

"But why?" Stu wondered aloud. "After what you went through to get it ... "

"It's all about listening to the automobile. And that doesn't mean paying attention to *sounds*. In fact, in my line of work—in most lines of work, I imagine—sounds are actually a distraction. With my implant removed, I can focus solely on the car, and give it the level of detail I know it deserves."

Stu was unconsciously leaning toward Alfred, fascinated by the car detailer's recounting of his personal and professional journey.

"Your professor," Stu inquired. "Does he . . . do any kind of private consultation?"

Alfred shook his head, eyes growing sad and dark. "Unfortunately, he passed away several years ago. But I value what he taught me so much, I keep it alive in my work, in my relationships, and in the conversations I have—like this one."

Stu nodded silently, and wondered if this was an opportunity he should pursue. *Alfred doesn't look like anyone who I would consider a mentor. But . . . if listening is his strength, maybe I should give him a try. Besides, what do I have to lose?*

"What's the most valuable thing you learned from Dr. Grove?" Stu asked.

"That's an easy one," Alfred said. "Dr. Grove taught me that 'listening is the core of living.' Why, I even pass along his favorite saying when I speak to people about him: *Listening pays in many ways . . . if you make the investment!*"

Stu smiled, nodding his head.

Alfred smiled back, but his eyes were cautious, probing. "Stu . . . who are you not listening to?" he asked.

Stu was surprised with the suddenness—the intimacy—of his question. "Um . . . what do you mean?" he stammered.

Alfred's eyes sparkled. "If you weren't interested in learning more about listening, I don't think you would stand still to hear my whole life story, let alone lean in with your whole body!"

Stu smiled shyly. "Was I doing that?" he asked, suddenly embarrassed.

"Like I said," Alfred replied, "I'm an expert in body language."

"I'll have to remember that next time."

"Well ... think about it," Alfred said. "I wasn't kidding when I said I could help you."

"I know," Stu replied.

Stu paid Alfred for the detailing, and reflected on what he had learned as he watched the spotless white detailing van drive away. *I can only imagine what it's like to see listening as a gift. Based on what I've been through this past week, it seems more like a curse!*

CHAPTER 6
Maturity Gap

Stu sat at a corner table of the busy coffee house, waiting for Brad Chappelle, his youngest sales manager. He finished off his plain black coffee and glanced at his watch. It was 10:19 a.m. The meeting had been scheduled for ten o'clock.

He checked his phone and saw the same text message that Brad had sent fifteen minutes earlier: *I'm on my way.* Stu looked out the window again, and then, at last, saw Brad's car pulling into the parking lot.

Stu had known Brad for only about two years, but he felt a deep obligation toward the young man. It had been Stu's decision to put Brad into the role of sales manager of the Wallsey branch—the position that opened up when Stu was promoted to regional sales director. Against Carl's suggestion to fill the position with someone who was "next in line," Stu decided to gamble on Brad, who was new to the organization but had a natural talent for sales. Stu thought that Brad could sell just about anything to anyone.

Brad was tall, athletic, and good-looking—and fully aware of the power that came with his appearance. He'd been drafted into professional baseball straight out of college, but turned down a minor league career to go into acting and modeling. After he found out that guys with his looks were a dime-a-dozen in Hollywood, he decided to go into sales instead, since there was less competition. Brad had persuasive charm but was undisciplined in his sales approach. Stu thought he could mentor the young man who he affectionately referred to as "the kid," and help him grow into an effective manager.

But soon enough, Stu discovered that success in sales doesn't necessarily translate into an ability to manage. From the moment Brad was promoted, there were problems. Two of the branch's most talented sales reps left the company, and those who stayed behind openly questioned Brad's abilities. Morale suffered and Stu increasingly heard rumblings of discontent. Brad complained to Stu that he was managing a bunch of "dinosaurs," apparently not noticing or caring that Stu himself had developed the same people into a successful team. Stu took the criticism personally. *I built that team into a powerhouse and he's letting it fall apart; he's got some nerve knocking my decisions.*

Because he knew the Wallsey branch so well, Stu didn't buy the argument that Brad needed "new blood" on the team—that sounded like an excuse. But with sales dropping and Brad's dissatisfaction growing, something needed to be done. Stu hoped today's impromptu meeting could help to prevent the problems from getting out of control.

Stu was reluctant to admit how disappointed he was in Brad's performance. At the same time, he felt a nagging resentment toward Brad's relaxed attitude and slow development. *I hired him, and I've still got high hopes for him. He's got so much talent and potential, but it's like he doesn't know what to do with it. Youth is wasted on the young. . . .*

Brad strolled into the coffee house like he was arriving at a red-carpet movie premiere. Today he was sporting thick black sunglasses beneath his styled hair, a black suit jacket over a gray silk shirt, no tie and two open buttons, with matching black pants and thick-soled black dress shoes that managed to make him look even taller.

Stu considered standing up or waving to help reveal his presence to his DynaCorp colleague, but he decided against it. *Brad is no dummy; he'll find me soon enough.*

Brad got in line to order, then spent several minutes flirting with the cute barista. Stu watched as the young lady batted her eyes and flipped her hair. Then the girl giggled so loudly at one of Brad's jokes that patrons at several tables looked over, clearly distracted by the show.

Ten minutes later Brad finally sauntered over to Stu's table, with the barista's phone number neatly written on the cardboard sleeve of his coffee cup.

"Thanks for agreeing to drive out here, Stu," Brad said sincerely, resting his sunglasses gently atop his head.

"Thanks for meeting me more than halfway, Brad," Stu said diplomatically.

He waited for Brad to apologize for being late and, upon being late, taking so long to play with the barista. Instead, Brad sat casually, and quietly slipped off his jacket and draped it over the back of his chair. Then he began sipping his coffee and looking around the room, then at others in the room, then casually back at Stu. "What did you want to see me about?"

Stu fumed. *Doesn't he know how to hold a proper business meeting? No wonder the kid can't run his own branch; he can barely show up on time and invest in a meeting with his own boss!*

Stu held his tongue, not wanting to ruin the meeting before it even started. The memory of last week's failed encounter with Rachel still bothered him. In fact, part of the reason he had wanted to meet with Brad was to send the message to all of his people: there was a new Stu in town, one who was eager to set things right. *It's hard to stay focused on being "the new Stu" . . . the kid isn't making this easy.*

"I'm just following up on our meeting earlier this month."

Finally, Stu had the younger man's attention. "Wow, really?" Brad asked, eyes wide as he tested his still hot coffee.

Stu smiled. "Is that so surprising?"

Brad looked back with intense eyes.

"Actually, yeah, it is. I mean, I've been asking you to help me with my sales force for months now and . . . nothing's happened yet, so . . . yeah, I'm real surprised."

Stu didn't let his irritation show. Instead, he blinked three times slowly—his version of "counting to ten"—and said, quite calmly, "You know, Brad, *you* are the sales manager at your branch. You shouldn't have to wait on me to act. Part of your role as manager is to solve problems, to come up with your own solutions."

"I tried that," Brad protested, his chiseled face looking visibly annoyed.

Stu replied without thinking. "Not in a way that I can tell. I mean, every meeting you give me the same thing: 'My sales staff is too old, they're dinosaurs, they're computer illiterate.' On and on it goes. I know these people can deliver because they used to report to me, and we were a winning team! But who manages the team now, Brad? You do. If you don't like what's going on, then do what it takes to fix it."

Brad huffed. "That's where you're wrong." His voice became strained. "I didn't hire these people; I *inherited* them. You didn't like the candidates I selected for the open positions, so that leaves two open positions on my team, and a bunch of old folks who are set in their ways and won't listen to anything I say. I would fire most of them if I could . . . "

Stu shook his head; he'd come here to be patient, kind, even generous with his time, but now Brad was pushing all the wrong buttons.

"Brad," Stu pointed out, more gruffly than he'd intended. "Your role as manager is to get them to listen to what you say."

"And *your* role as sales director is to listen to what *I'm* saying: *they won't listen to me.* I need your help. Am I proud of it? No, but . . . wouldn't you rather have me come to *you* for help . . . instead of me going to Carl?"

"Frankly, I wouldn't prefer either of those options. If you were a teacher and I was your principal, what would you do? If you couldn't control the kids in your classroom, would you ask me to kick them all out and just . . . start over? No, you'd take back control and solve this problem for yourself."

"So what's the point of this meeting?" Brad spewed. "What's the point of having a leader if he can't . . . or won't . . . *lead*? You're all about praising me when sales are up, taking credit, pointing out how well things are going . . . but if I need your help, you wash your hands completely. What's up with that?"

"Maybe you need to listen to the old folks in your branch," Stu shot back. "With age comes experience. When I was in your position, I would have never thought to talk back to my supervisor. *Never!* I would have just buckled down and gotten the job done . . . because that's what was expected of me. The problem with you is that you want everything handed to you. You want a solution from me, but you're not willing to do anything about it!"

Brad glared. "How would you know what I've done about it?" He took a breath and continued. "It's been ages since you've driven all the way down to my branch. You'll drive all the way to see Rachel, but not me? And for the record, I have tried to handle my own business. I wanted to solve my own problems and be a self-starter, but I came up against a team that was determined to see me fail. When I saw that I was going to need some help, I came to you as a last resort. You know what message you're sending to my staff? That you don't care; that corporate doesn't care. That I'm on my own, and no one's got my back—and that gives them the freedom to walk all over me. So not only are you not helping, you're actively making things worse."

At that moment, Brad's mobile phone rang. Without hesitation, he answered the call, standing and stepping away from the table.

While Brad was preoccupied, Stu sighed and held his hand to his forehead. *The kid has missed my point entirely.*

Brad clicked off his phone and turned back to Stu. "I'm sorry, but it looks like I've got an important client meeting I need to get to." With false sincerity, he added, "Thanks for coming out to meet me."

With that, Brad snatched his jacket off the back of his chair and walked out of the shop without a backward glance at Stu, or even at the pretty barista.

Stu watched Brad exit. In the silence that followed Brad's departure, Stu noticed that his pulse was pounding and his palms were a bit clammy. Two or three weeks ago, he would have written off an encounter like this as the cost of doing business. But now the stakes were higher. His business—or, at least, his job with DynaCorp Plastics—was on the line. Suddenly he was at the mercy of his employees, rather than the other way around. *There's no telling what Rachel said to Carl about our little blowup last week. Now, if Brad was to call Carl and pile on his complaints—I could get axed before the six-month deadline.*

Stu sat, quietly fuming . . . and worrying. Clearly, this approach of just trying harder wasn't getting the job done. Sales were down, not up. His people were more disappointed and disgusted with him, not less. *I gotta do something . . . something different . . . I need a plan.*

Stu sighed. As he stared out the windows, a long, dark limousine hurried past. The gleam of the car was flawless, well-polished; it made him immediately think of Alfred—strong, experienced, capable, and calm Alfred—with his spotless white overalls and simple business model and his expertise in listening. *Alfred could be the answer. If not the answer, he at least might be able to provide some tips.*

Stu knew he wasn't due for another appointment with Alfred until the end of the month. But, he reasoned, this was an emergency. As a man who values listening, surely Alfred would understand Stu's need.

He slid open his phone and called Alfred's number.

"Hello . . . Alfred? This is Stu Preston. I hope you don't mind me making an appointment on short notice . . . "

CHAPTER 7
Trouble at Home

Stu was simultaneously driving his car and talking to his wife Jennifer on his phone when he spotted the D'Amato Detailing van, sitting alone on an outer edge of the shopping mall parking lot. Alfred, dressed in his white uniform, was seated in a folding lawn chair only a few feet away, enjoying the cool sunshine of a Tuesday afternoon.

Stu continued his phone conversation as he parked the car, stepped out, and waved at the older gentleman.

Alfred stood and gave a nod.

As Stu walked over to the van, he wrapped up the call with Jennifer. "Okay, babe . . . yeah, that sounds like a plan . . . okay . . . bye."

The two men greeted each other, shaking hands warmly.

Although he had not been parked there more than a minute, already Stu noticed several drivers on their way to the busy mall who were slowing down to check out the auto detailer's striking white van.

"Now, Alfred . . . tell me again why we agreed to meet here?"

Alfred winked and said, "Well, it's a beautiful day, and it never hurts to be outside and get some fresh air . . . and a little free advertising."

"You sure you didn't minor in advertising?" Stu said, teasing him.

"No, but I got a crash course in it once I started my detailing business, that's for sure." Alfred smiled. He moved over to examine Stu's car. "Well, let's take a look at her."

Alfred circled the Porsche, carefully studying its sleek, black finish. "I don't know," he said with a bemused expression. "I don't see what all the urgency is about. This car looks pretty clean to me."

Stu looked intensely into Alfred's eyes and confessed, "Well, since you mentioned it . . . the car is not my biggest problem today. I . . . called you because I think I might need a little help in the listening department."

Alfred cocked one graying eyebrow. "Really?"

Stu didn't respond; he was still trying to find the right words.

Alfred gently nudged. "What's going on?"

Stu leaned against his car and said, "I don't know where else to turn. My job is on the line. I've never been in this kind of situation before."

"Is your job really on the line? Or is that just your interpretation?"

"I wish it wasn't, but . . . just last week my boss told me that I have six months to turn my job performance around. If I don't . . . it's over. I guess there are other places I could go, but I've worked at DynaCorp my whole career. I don't want to have to start all over again somewhere else."

Alfred shook his head and crossed his arms over his chest. "I'm not sure I see what your boss sees. You seem professional to me. I can't imagine you being any other way."

"I don't think it's professionalism that I have a problem with. Or maybe it is . . . I'm not sure anymore."

"What did the boss say you need to work on, specifically?" Alfred asked.

As he remembered Carl's words, Stu frowned and looked down in embarrassment. "He said I don't listen well . . . that I'm not paying attention to the needs of my employees."

Alfred nodded, then paused. "Is that how you see it?"

"I didn't before, "Stu answered. "But once he mentioned it . . . and I saw how hard it was to take care of it on my own . . . I think I'm starting to believe him."

Alfred nodded again, and smiled. "So what brought you here today?"

Stu sighed. "I thought you said you were a great listener."

The older man smirked, and added, "I meant, specifically, *today*. What made you pick up the phone *today* and call me a week and a half before your next appointment?"

"I just had a meeting with one of my branch sales managers. I went into it prepared to be patient, understanding, empathetic. In short, *to listen*. But the minute this kid opened his mouth, I couldn't help myself. I just laid into him, and needless to say, the meeting went down from there. I panicked, figuring he'd run and tell my boss right away. And then I called you."

Alfred nodded and reached into his pocket to take out a simple notepad. He flipped it open and began scribbling out a few lines.

"Please tell me that's a prescription to solve my problem!" Stu blurted.

Alfred chuckled, the lines around his eyes wrinkling. "Not quite. I'm just jotting down some notes. How about you meet me back here in two days and I'll have some material ready for you?"

"Material?"

"Dr. Grove shared his entire system with me. It has some simple tools that I think you'll find quite useful. But I want to make sure I pick the right ones."

Stu couldn't hide his disappointment. "You mean, there's more than one?"

Alfred smiled dryly, writing a few more notes. "I think I'm starting to see the root of your problem."

Stu was intrigued. "Really? What do you think it is?"

"Wanting a simple solution," Alfred said.

Stu shook his head. "Isn't there anything you can give me today?"

"Sure," said Alfred. "I'll offer a piece of advice."

Stu looked at Alfred blankly. "Okay . . . ?"

Alfred spoke deliberately. *"First, you have to commit."*

Stu waited to see if there was more. The old man looked at him with pure serenity.

"That's it?"

"That's a start," Alfred said, smiling. He checked his notebook again. "So . . . Thursday afternoon?

Stu checked his phone. "Uh . . . yeah, that should work."

Alfred politely excused himself to get moving on to his next detailing appointment. The two men shook hands and said their goodbyes.

As Stu watched the white van drive away, he shook his head and let out a sigh of disgust.

• • •

As Stu drove home later that evening, his mind raced in a swirl of frustration. He'd been looking for a simple fix and hadn't gotten it. Instead he'd been told he'd have to wait two days, and then he'd only be at the beginning of what seemed to be a drawn-out solution. *I didn't get what I asked for, and that advice was baffling. But I have to do something and I'm running out of options.*

"Stu?" his wife called from the kitchen as he entered the house. He found Jennifer nibbling on a piece of cheese. "What took you so long?" she asked.

Stu deposited his laptop bag on a kitchen barstool and looked up to see that his wife was standing in the shadow.

There was only one light on over the sink, and the rest of the kitchen was quiet and empty.

"Huh?" he stammered. "I thought I told you, I was getting my car detailed, and then I had to go back to the office."

Jennifer's eyes narrowed; she wasn't the kind to take throwaway excuses without a fight.

Still, he resisted the urge to tell her much about what was going on at work—with Carl, with his staff, most certainly with Alfred. *Jennifer doesn't need to know about any of this.*

"Again?" she asked carefully. "How dirty can your car get sitting in the parking garage all day?"

"I don't just sit around all day," he snapped. He opened the refrigerator to reach for a beer and leaned against the counter across from her.

"I didn't say *you* did. I said your *car* did. Anyway, it's fine; you do what you want, I just . . . you said you'd bring home dinner and that was hours ago."

"What?" Stu blurted. "I never said that." *No way would I promise to bring home dinner on a Tuesday night.*

Jennifer's eyes narrowed again. "Do you think I've been drinking? I was talking to you on the phone about what you wanted for dinner. You said that you were at the mall and would pick up something on the way home!" She glared at him.

Stu sighed. "I totally blanked on that, babe. I'm sorry. Can't we just whip up something out of the freezer?"

"We?" she retorted. "Don't you mean *me*, Stu?" Her jaw clenched for a moment. "Forget it; I've got the number for Luigi's, I'll just order something from them." She snatched a battered take-out menu from a stack on the kitchen counter and scanned it in exasperation.

"It's just dinner," he offered, sounding half-apologetic, half-defensive.

"It's *not* just dinner," she snapped. "It's *everything*. You make me feel like *I'm* going crazy . . . questioning me about things *I know* you said. How is that supposed to make me feel? To be treated like I'm not important enough for you to listen to?"

"It's not that," he insisted, inching forward. "You are important, babe, it's just . . . I have a lot going on at work."

"And I don't?" she blurted, her face darkening as she clutched the phone. "My work is every bit as important as yours, but how often do you ask me how *my* day went? Do you care about when Jimmy Robinson is getting his cast taken off? Or those motivational bookmarks I ordered for the Reading Club?"

She paused. Stu stared at her expressionless, blinking.

"Look at your face now, Stu; you have no idea who— or *what*—I'm even talking about. I might as well be speaking a foreign language."

Jennifer stood silently, the menu in one hand, the phone in the other, eyeing him. There was a quiver in her breath.

Stu said nothing. *What can I say? That she's right? And that I know it?*

Jennifer slammed the phone down onto the charger, flung the menu onto the counter, and grabbed her purse. She headed for the garage.

"Where are you going?" he asked.

"Caroline asked me to join her for dinner earlier, but I turned her down because you said you were bringing something home. I hope I'm not too late to meet up with her."

"What about me?" he asked. As soon as the words left his mouth, he regretted it.

Jennifer rolled her eyes and sneered, "Didn't you say you wanted to whip something up from the freezer? Now's your chance!"

Despite her anger, she carefully pulled the door behind her without slamming it. Stu heard the car start, then the automatic garage door opened . . . and closed. And then, silence.

CHAPTER 8
Build a Solid Foundation

When his two days of waiting were finally up, Stu raced to meet Alfred at a nearby coffee shop. As he parked the car, he noted how odd it felt to be meeting Alfred for something other than car detailing. He walked in and saw that Alfred was waiting patiently for him, with his high-tech earpiece resting on a napkin as he sipped contentedly at a cup of tea.

Stu ordered impatiently, barely noticing what he was doing. He picked up his iced coffee and carefully walked around the table to take a seat across from Alfred, not wanting to startle him.

Alfred nodded, as if he'd known Stu was there all along, and silently, expertly slid in his cochlear implant.

"Don't you like to hear what's going on around you?" Stu asked curiously.

"Sometimes silence is better," Alfred pointed out. He tapped a small purple folder next to his empty cup. "Are you ready for your first lesson?"

"I guess so." Stu knew he needed the help, but he was still a bit uncertain about what he was getting himself into.

Alfred nodded and opened the folder. Inside it were several multi-colored cards, each printed on heavy stock and about the size of a large postcard.

"I can't teach you the entire fifteen-week course, so I thought I would go through my notes and give you the best of the best material that Dr. Grove provided. I've created a series of what I call 'listening aids'—not hearing aids, but listening aids."

Stu tried to follow along, though he found the idea of "listening aids" rather strange.

Alfred continued. "Today, I will give you the road map and we will also dive into the first lesson." He took a card from the folder and handed it to Stu. "This is Dr. Grove's 'Listening Pays' system. He said that he compressed forty years of listening practice, teaching, and research into this hexagonal figure."

Alfred paused to let Stu examine the card.

"The Listening Pays system consists of six simple and practical strategies.[1] They are all connected, and the atom in the middle represents energy—*your energy*—flowing through them. The strategies work together, and they are constantly in motion. He called it 'Listening Pays' because of the tremendous payoff that comes through the power of listening. He also emphasized that it is a lifetime process. As Dr. Grove used to say, 'Listening pays in many ways, because you make the investment.'"

Stu pondered what he had just heard. *Maybe listening really can pay . . . or, at least, help me save my job.*

LISTENING PAYS

Achieve Significance through the Power of Listening

Six Strategies

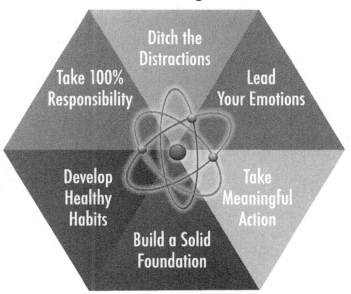

Take 100% Responsibility

Ditch the Distractions

Lead Your Emotions

Develop Healthy Habits

Build a Solid Foundation

Take Meaningful Action

©2012, Dr. Rick Bommelje

After a moment, Alfred continued. "When combined together, these six strategies help you achieve significance."

"What does that mean?" Stu asked, pointing to the subtitle. "How does listening help 'achieve significance'?"

"Well . . . it's really up to you to decide that," Alfred replied.

Stu looked up at Alfred and blinked. *We're only two minutes into the first lesson and already I'm confused.*

Alfred, picking up on Stu's discomfort, continued. "The meaning of 'significance' will be different for each person. It might mean conquering a special goal, fulfilling your fullest potential . . . finding meaning and joy, living in alignment with your purpose . . . or repairing a broken relationship. Whatever kind of significance you are seeking, listening can help you find it. Essentially, listening is living—the quality of your listening is equal to the quality of your life."

Alfred paused again to let Stu take in his message. When Stu looked at him and nodded, he continued. "Each time we meet, we will focus on one of these six strategies. Your job will be to study the strategy, learn it, and put it into action.

The six strategies are:

1. Build a Solid Foundation

2. Develop Healthy Habits

3. Take 100% Responsibility

4. Ditch the Distractions

5. Lead Your Emotions

6. Take the Meaningful Action"

Alfred waited to get Stu's full attention before continuing. "Are you ready to get started with the first strategy?"

"Yes, let's continue," Stu said, smiling.

"Excellent. The first strategy is to *Build a Solid Foundation*. This strategy is referred to as the foundation because it is at the core of the entire system. There is one main point to this strategy, and that is to define listening.

"In all of Dr. Grove's years of studying listening, he encountered many definitions for 'listening.' However, he found there is only one that covers every possible part of the listening process. He called it SIER*... that's right; it sounds like the word *clear*... SIER* with an asterisk. When you break it down, listening is a dynamic process consisting of five vital stages."

Build a Solid Foundation

Listening = SIER*

S ENSE

- Use all of your senses to take in the message: hear it, see it, smell it, taste it, touch it.
- Recognize not only what people say, but how they say it and show it.

I NTERPRET

- Withhold judgement until your understanding is complete.
- Encourage the speaker to keep speaking.
- Clarify your understanding of the message (ask questions, repeat back in your own words, summarize and check for agreement).

E VALUATE

- Test the message against the evidence available.
- Probe with follow-up questions to deepen understanding.
- Identify if the message is a fact, an opinion, or a prediction.
- Take time to discern, to be confident that you have intentionally evaluated.
- Decide your response.

R ESPOND

- Recognize that how you respond is not only what you say, but how you say it and show it.
- Before responding, ask yourself: "Will my response add value?" (If the answer is no, adjust what you say or show.)
- Take care to respond rather than react.
- Share your response with conscious intent.

* M E M O R Y

If you choose to bring information into long term memory, consciously move it through each stage in the process.

LISTENING AID #1A

Alfred reached into his folder and pulled out Listening Aid 1A.

"SIER* stands for *Sense, Interpret, Evaluate,* and *Respond.*" Alfred pointed to each of the words as he said them. And the asterisk stands for *Memory.*"[2]

Stu took a breath. While everything he heard was making sense, it was all so new and different that it took real effort for him to focus on Alfred's words.

The older man looked up at Stu and said, "From this moment on, whenever you think of the word *listen* or *listening,* immediately think about what you see on this card: SIER*. Refer to this card frequently, because this is a big deal. I want you to keep it handy."

Stu was eager to learn, but he grew concerned as he realized how much time and effort this was going to take. "Sounds good . . . but can't you just give me the rest of the listening aids and let me work ahead?"

Alfred shook his head. "I appreciate your enthusiasm . . . but it's not quite that easy. Listening isn't about gaining some quick knowledge and passing a test. The fact is, listening requires you to go beyond mere knowledge; you must make it an ongoing daily practice in order to master it."

Stu sighed, his face showing his unease.

Alfred's tone softened. "It's not impossible, and once you get started, you'll see results right away," he said. "And I'm looking forward to guiding you through each strategy."

"Okay," Stu sighed, sliding away his quickly forgotten coffee to focus on the card in his hand. "So...what comes first?"

Alfred nodded patiently and began, "With SIER*, each stage is essential and, to get the greatest value, you have to do them in order.

"The first stage of the listening process is to *sense*. Effective listeners focus first on fully taking in a sender's messages using all of their senses: sound, sight, smell, taste, and touch.

"After you have sensed the message, you have earned the right to proceed to the second step, *interpret*. This is about interpreting, or understanding, the speaker's message correctly so that it matches the speaker's intent. You can ask yourself the basic questions: Do the words mean the same to both of us? Are we talking about the same thing?

"In interpreting the message, it's important to remember to withhold your judgment until you fully understand what the speaker is trying to say. This can be very challenging. The fact is, most people have made a judgment about what someone is saying, or even about the speaker himself, before that person is through talking. In the fast-paced world we live in, many people are unaware of how much they want to talk more and listen less.

"Only after you have completed the first two stages can you properly move on to the next stage: *evaluate* the message. You can then decide whether you like or dislike, agree or disagree with, accept or reject the speaker's message. This is where you make judgments about what you are interpreting.

"The fourth stage is *respond*. This stage is often overlooked in the listening process. This means actually taking action. It is what you say or what you show nonverbally. There is a big difference between *responding* and *reacting*. Responding is leading your emotions, while reacting is being swept up with your emotions and letting them lead you."

Alfred paused to make sure that he hadn't overwhelmed Stu with too much information.

After a moment, Stu asked, "What does 'memory' have to do with it?"

Alfred smiled as if he had anticipated the question. "All of these four stages are connected together by 'memory,' or remembering. This is the asterisk. By consciously moving through each stage in the process, you deposit what you want to into your long-term memory bank."

Stu nodded, although he felt like there was a lot more to remembering than simply making a "deposit" in his "memory bank."

"There is one more crucial point in SIER*," Alfred concluded, "which is the time factor." He turned the card over to reveal Listening Aid 1B, which showed a simple picture of a large hourglass.

"The hourglass represents how you spend your time . . . it represents your life," Alfred explained. "The sand in the top is your future; the sand in the bottom is your past. The grains of sand flowing through the tube

Build a Solid Foundation

Time Opportunities to Apply SIER*

SIER* can be applied to your interactions in various ways.

 ### In the FUTURE:
Use SIER* to plan and develop your approach to important interactions.

 ### In the PRESENT:
Use SIER* to apply and deliver effective listening skills to be more effective in the moment.

 ### In the PAST:
Use SIER* to debrief your effectiveness and to diagnose communication problems.

Adapted from *Listening Leaders* by
Dr. Lyman K. Steil & Dr. Richard K. Bommelje

LISTENING AID #1B

©2012, Dr. Rick Bommelje

represent the present moment, otherwise known as the 'now.' SIER*ing occurs in the moment. The challenge is for you to constantly keep your consciousness in the present—to *be here now.*

"However, the awareness that comes from SIER*ing can also help you examine your listening effectiveness in the past, and prepare for interactions in the future."

Alfred gathered up the first two cards and tucked them back inside the folder. Then he pulled out the next listening aid, which was labeled "Daily Listening Scorecard."

Stu gave Alfred a questioning look and said, "What do I do with this?"

Alfred smiled, leaning back in his seat. "This will be your homework for the next two weeks."

Stu looked up, speechless. Alfred explained. "The Daily Listening Scorecard is a tool that will raise your listening awareness on a daily basis. This is important, because all growth begins with awareness. Your assignment is to check yourself every day, and identify the number of times you violate SIER* by engaging these behaviors. Then at the end of each day, transfer your numbers to the form on the back. It is very important to track your results in writing. Don't do it in your head."

Stu flipped the listening aid over and saw another grid printed on the back of the card—the Weekly Listening Scorecard.

"When you record zeroes for any of the nine items, you will know that you are making great progress. Study your results at the end of each day and see which item is

Build a Solid Foundation

Daily Listening Scorecard

Throughout the day, record the number of times you violate SIER*
by engaging in the following behaviors.

Number of
Instances

SENSE

1. Stopped making eye contact with
the speaker _____

2. Asked someone to repeat himself/
herself because I was not focusing _____

INTERPRET

3. Misunderstood the meaning of
someone's message _____

4. Let my mind wander while someone
was speaking _____

EVALUATE

5. Jumped to a conclusion about what
someone was going to say _____

6. Let my personal judgments crowd
out the speaker's message _____

RESPOND

7. Interrupted someone or changed the
subject in the middle of the conversation _____

8. Reacted emotionally to what someone
was saying before they finished _____

MEMORY

9. Forgot important information
(such as a person's name) while
communicating with someone _____

©2012, Dr. Rick Bommelje   **LISTENING AID #2A**

84

being repeated the most often. Then make a conscious effort to focus on this item the next day. At the end of the week, you'll be able to see your progress."

"So I just do this for one week?" Stu asked.

"At least one week," Alfred said. "Some students fill it out every day for a month."

Stu glanced back at the card.

Alfred continued. "I challenge you to learn SIER* inside and out. Study the listening aid and begin to put each of the stages into practice. The stages happen very, very fast—like the snap of a finger. But when you are intentionally thinking about how you are listening—or SIER*ing—you will create value for yourself and others, too.

"One other way to approach SIER* is to think about it as an acronym for *success in each relationship*—or in your field it could even stand for a *sale in each relationship.*"

Stu scratched his head as Alfred wound down his first lesson.

"So, what do you think?" Alfred asked.

"Well," Stu said quietly, his voice sounding a bit intimidated, "there is a whole lot more to this listening stuff than I thought there would be."

Alfred smiled until his eyes crinkled. "Aren't you glad you finally got started? We're just scratching the surface!"

Build a Solid Foundation

Weekly Listening Scorecard

*Track your progress and raise awareness of your
negative listening behaviors.*

*Throughout the week, transfer scores from your daily listening
scorecards to record the number of times you exhibit
the following behaviors.*

	Sun	Mon	Tue	Wed	Thu	Fri	Sat
Stopped eye contact							
Asked for repeat							
Misunderstood							
Mind wandered							
Jumped to conclusion							
Let judgement crowd out message							
Interrupted							
Reacted emotionally							
Forgot important information							

LISTENING AID #2B

CHAPTER 9
SIER*

The next morning, Stu sat in the crowded coffeehouse across the street from his office building. Even though he was running a little behind schedule, he felt the need to stop in for some caffeine; he'd lost sleep overnight pondering his probation and how to apply what he was learning from Alfred.

He sipped his coffee and looked closely at his SIER* listening aid.

Stu realized that before he met Alfred, he'd been stumbling along blindly in the wake of Carl's mandate. He had tried to listen better on his own, but that hadn't worked out. He thought listening amounted to making eye contact and acting like you were paying attention to others. But it was becoming clear to Stu that listening—*really* listening—required much more.

Stu thought back to his recent meetings with Rachel and Brad. His intention was to try to smooth things over with them, to make it look like he was mending his ways.

Instead, he got so upset with what they were saying that he not only stopped listening, he blew up at them. He saw that his behaviors weren't just bringing his communication to a standstill; he was actually doing damage to his relationships.

Now he had a system to use; an actual set of strategies for improving his communication—from a student of a proven listening expert, no less. *I've got six months to shape up. I'll either learn it now, or I'll learn it the hard way later.*

He had to admit: he wasn't sure he could learn and apply all the concepts and skills, and show results before his six-month deadline. But at the same time, he had total trust in Alfred D'Amato. *I can't doubt Alfred's intentions, or that he knows what he's talking about. I hope this turns out to be the right solution for me.*

He stared silently at the SIER* card, and remembered the sound of Alfred's voice, explaining that "all growth begins with awareness." *Awareness . . . I've always considered myself pretty "aware," but according to my boss, my direct reports, and even my wife, it looks like I'm anything but.*

On the SIER* card, he saw the word *SENSE* staring back at him from the top line. He decided to start there. *Use all of your senses . . . hear it, see it, smell it, taste it, touch it.*

Stu nodded, as if hearing Alfred's voice in his head. He put the card away and focused on his surroundings. He smiled as he looked around. *If there was ever a time and place to indulge the senses—all the senses—it was in a crowded coffee shop on a weekday morning.*

He saw the baristas behind the busy cash register, mostly young people, probably college kids working before a late-morning class. They looked a bit harried and rushed, but not unhappy. He was amused to think about the various odd jobs he had done in his late teens and early twenties, before the responsibilities of adulthood took over his life.

He turned his attention to the line of customers. He noticed that collectively, they looked impatient and distracted. A woman wearing a gray business suit and smart glasses was having an animated conversation on her mobile phone. A tall man in a shirt and tie was reading the newspaper, ignoring everything else around him as he inched forward. A pretty young college student held a little dog in a carrier strapped over her shoulders, while an older couple dressed in jogging suits made faces at the pup, and chatted pleasantly with the girl.

Stu watched as the man with the newspaper moved over to the serving counter. The gentleman was so absorbed in his paper, the barista called his name three times before he looked up to take his coffee. Stu smiled to himself. *I wonder if that's how I look when I'm focused on my text messages.*

The store was full of rich smells as well; the aroma of fresh-brewed coffee, the hint of cinnamon and nutmeg from the condiment stand nearby, the scent of baked goods in the display case, even the odd waft of aftershave or perfume as the city's single young professionals strode in and out.

Stu began focusing on the sounds; he noted that there were many to sift through. First, there was some bluesy, soft rock drifting from the overhead speakers. It was too low to tell who or what the band was, and not good enough for him to care. Then there was the hissing of the cappuccino maker, the gurgling of the regular coffee brewers, the clinking of spoons twirling in white ceramic mugs.

Everywhere there was conversation. The woman in the gray business suit had received her order, but continued to talk on her mobile phone. She stood over Stu's shoulder, stirring honey into her tea, and complained into her phone that "those figures were late because of Lynn, and I'm not taking the blame this time. You tell her that when I get there, I'll ... "

The pet-loving college girl picked up her coffee and bent to look her little dog directly in the eye. "Not much longer now, Roxie; we'll get to the playground soon."

Then the older couple brought their morning drinks to a table next to Stu. They were sitting so close their knees were almost touching. He had a bike cap over what appeared to be a bald head, and she wore pink socks with her brand new jogging shoes. Their voices were quite strained as they quietly argued.

"We were just talking ... about the dog," he said emphatically. "She was only being friendly with me!"

The woman leaned in and said, just as earnestly, "I don't care what *that girl* was doing ... *you* were making a fool of yourself!" Stu suppressed a laugh and looked away, too polite to eavesdrop.

He felt like he was finally in a good state of aware- ness; that he was using his *senses* to grasp what was going on around him. He pulled out the SIER* card for one last tip. *Recognize not only what people say, but how they say it and show it.*

He put the card away, bid a silent farewell to the quarreling couple, and walked across the street to his office.

He had a full day ahead, with all the usual duties to attend to, but no deadlines. Stu decided it was the perfect kind of day to devote to SIER*ing and raising his aware- ness. He was wondering where he might start when he heard the muffled voice of his assistant, Linda, speaking on her mobile phone.

Stu stopped outside the office and looked at his watch; it was nearly 8:45. *It's not like Linda to be on her personal phone during business hours. And that's her rule, not the company's.*

Through the frosted glass that led to his outer office, Stu saw that Linda's face was tense, troubled, as she stared blankly out the small window behind her desk. In profile, her stooped posture conveyed a sense of concern, as if she were carrying a weight on her shoulders.

He thought of the SIER* listening aid in his pocket and what it had said about *sense*: *Recognize not only what people say, but how they say it and show it.* He decided to put the technique to the test, right then and there, with Linda.

As he made his way through the outer office door, he scuffed his feet a bit and cleared his throat to make his presence known. Linda was just hanging up her phone and they greeted each other with smiles.

"Good morning, Stu," she said brightly, without a hint of the previous tension in her voice.

"Morning, Linda," he said, pausing at his office door. "Do you mind stepping in here so we can chat for a few seconds?"

She stood cautiously. Stu rarely called her into his office. That was because most of the time, she was already lurking there, whether she'd been invited or not.

"Anything wrong?" she asked hesitantly, sinking into the leather chair across from his cluttered desk.

"Not with me," he sighed, sitting back. "But you seem . . . tense . . . this morning."

"I do?" she asked.

Rather than answer right away, Stu continued to watch. He was at the "I" stage of SIER* as he tried to interpret Linda's verbal and non-verbal statements.

He watched how Linda was sitting—too upright for her usual carefree posture. Her rectangular glasses were up close against her eyes and high on her nose, as if she'd been shoving them up all morning. Her clothes, as always, were neat. But she was wearing the same jewelry she'd worn earlier that week; Stu remembered because he had commented on the necklace. He wasn't sure, but he thought that Linda tried to wear something different each day of the week. Her hair was clean but not as straight as usual. He knew it was humid outside this morning, but Linda usually took a little more time with her hair than that.

Stu waited until the silence at last grew awkward. "You sure?" he asked.

"Sure," she said quickly. There was some uncertainty in her tone.

Stu was relishing how different the moment felt, noticing how intriguing it was to slow down and fully sense and interpret. He sat there, smiling peacefully, waiting.

The atmosphere grew at first tense, then ... confessional.

"What's with you this morning?" she asked, voice full of emotion.

"I'm trying something new," he confessed.

"Like what ... listening for a change?" she quipped.

He chuckled. "As a matter of fact, yes!"

She sighed, took a deep breath, and said, "Well, then I guess I'll give you something to listen to: my boyfriend is moving out!"

"What?" Stu asked, sitting up in his chair and planting his palms against the top of his desk. "But he just moved in!"

Linda's face melted into a mask of disbelief. "Stu, that was *two years ago*!"

Stu realized he still had quite a bit of work to do. He knew, instinctively, that he owed this moment to a breakdown at the asterisk level of SIER*, also known as "memory." Simply put, he knew he had failed to *remember* information he had been exposed to regularly for several years.

As Linda poured out her story, Stu continued practicing, working his way down the SIER* listening aid and back up again, trying to *sense, interpret, evaluate, respond,* and *remember.* At the end of the conversation, Linda felt better and Stu learned new things about his assistant that made him feel personally connected to her.

Throughout the rest of the day, Stu kept his SIER* card handy, and tried to be aware of each of the stages during his conversations. In addition, he completed his homework, tallying his SIER* violations on his daily listening scorecard.

At the end of his first full day of using the Listening Pays system, Stu's scorecard told him the day's most valuable lesson: that he had a lot more work to do if he was going to be a better listener.

Build a Solid Foundation

Daily Listening Scorecard

Throughout the day, record the number of times you violate SIER*
by engaging in the following behaviors.

		Number of Instances
SENSE	1. Stopped making eye contact with the speaker	3
	2. Asked someone to repeat himself/ herself because I was not focusing	
INTERPRET	3. Misunderstood the meaning of someone's message	
	4. Let my mind wander while someone was speaking	6
EVALUATE	5. Jumped to a conclusion about what someone was going to say	2
	6. Let my personal judgments crowd out the speaker's message	
RESPOND	7. Interrupted someone or changed the subject in the middle of the conversation	3
	8. Reacted emotionally to what someone was saying before they finished	3
MEMORY	9. Forgot important information (such as a person's name) while communicating with someone	4

LISTENING AID #2A

CHAPTER 10
The Path to Awareness

Stu finished the last of his lo mein noodles as he watched Charlie Hartman, sales manager at the Clark branch, sidle up to the buffet table for a third helping of dim sum.

They were just around the corner from Charlie's office at a convenient eatery called Ron's Won Ton Bar. This busy cafeteria-style restaurant, known for its all-you-can-eat buffet, was Charlie's favorite place to meet. The place was always crowded and noisy during the peak of the lunch rush. Stu, knowing this, scheduled his meeting with Charlie for 1:30 p.m., so the number of guests and the noise level would be at a minimum. He wanted to have Charlie's full attention, and for Charlie to have his.

While Charlie piled a few more peel-and-eat shrimp onto his plate, Stu pulled out his SIER* card and reminded himself of what each of the four letters meant:

Sense

Interpret

Evaluate

Respond

Charlie approached the table with another heaping meal and a smile on his face. Stu felt relaxed, open, and ready; he was ready for "awareness."

Charlie slid himself into the booth and adjusted his napkin. He deeply inhaled the mix of aromas coming from his plate and gave a look of gastronomic satisfaction. In between bites of food, he said, "I have to say, Stu, your call this morning surprised me."

"Why's that?" Stu offered gently, careful to make eye contact and take note of Charlie's relaxed body language.

Charlie grunted and said, "Well, it's not very often that you come all the way out here to my branch and ask me to lunch."

Stu nodded and said, "Why do you think that is, Charlie?"

Charlie paused, nibbling on a green bean. Then he said, "Well . . . I don't know . . . I suppose it's not always pleasant to hear bad news?"

Stu nodded, observing Charlie's questioning tone and slight smile. *Maybe Charlie is starting to figure out that his complaining is one of the reasons that I visit so rarely.*

Stu responded, "Good news or bad news, I'm trying to make myself more available to you."

Charlie's eyes widened at the comment and he pushed his plate away. His upper body shifted as he brought his right arm to rest across the back of the booth.

"I'm glad to hear that, Stu," Charlie murmured, eyes closing slightly. "Does this mean you're prepared to talk about pricing?"

Stu sighed, giving a look of calm resignation. "Time to get to the heart of the matter, right?"

"Well, I figured we didn't come here just for the won tons."

The two men shared a brief grin of acknowledgment. Then, Stu saw a kind of wave pass over Charlie's wide face; it was a look of concern he'd rarely seen before.

"Stu, I know you think I'm a pain in the butt, and—"

"Not at all, Charlie," Stu interrupted to make his point. "I just think that you've been obsessed about the pricing issue for . . . well, as long as you've reported to me."

Stu sensed Charlie's surprise at being interrupted. But this time Stu couldn't help it. *He goes on and on and we need to stay focused on the topic.* But then, Stu took a moment and forced himself to back off. He remembered what his handy SIER* card said: *"Encourage the speaker to keep speaking."*

"Why do you think that is, Stu?" Charlie said, his face growing darker. "I mean, have you ever in all our time working together heard me complain about anything else? That alone should tell you I'm serious about this issue. I'm not one to complain about just anything."

"Let's talk specifics," Stu blurted before Charlie could run the conversation into the ditch again. Stu was thinking of the "I" in SIER* and how to *interpret* what he was hearing; the method suggested that he *"clarify understanding of the message by asking questions."*

"What, exactly, is your specific complaint about pricing?" As he said it, Stu realized he'd never actually asked that question before.

Charlie blinked several times, clearly coming to the same realization.

"Well, you see . . . ," Charlie hemmed. "It's not so much the pricing, as the ability to negotiate. Before I joined DynaCorp, I worked for Breeze Solutions, the patio materials company. There, we had a 15 percent wiggle rate, where we could use some judgment without first seeking approval. It was our call to make, so long as we did it judiciously.

"Here at DynaCorp, my guys have got no latitude at the bargaining table; the price point is fixed and it seems like all the other salespeople at the competing plastics companies have—"

"Hold on," Stu stopped him again. "Can you name one of our competitors that doesn't have fixed price points?"

"Pulse Plastics, for one," Charlie said immediately. "I was having lunch with their top salesman, Phil, just the other day. He says it's standard for him to be able to slash prices 10 to 15 percent at the table . . . and without a call into headquarters."

Stu shook his head. "Charlie, the reason our price points are fixed is because we're already lower than Pulse Plastics. It's the same story with Kelly Plastics and Poly-Plex. Corporate made that decision years ago and regularly does price comparisons to keep it fixed. The system is designed to make it easier on you, Charlie; not harder."

Charlie was shaking his head now; his eyes shone with defiance.

"It might make it easier for the bean counters back at corporate, Stu, but you've been on the front lines; you know how valuable it can be during a negotiation to at least give the *appearance* that you're willing to negotiate. You guys are tying my hands with no real appreciation of what it's like."

"I know what it's like, Charlie, and there is a distinct advantage in staying firm."

Charlie shook his head again. "But not for some clients. You know that as well as I do. Some of these guys only want to do business with guys who will negotiate back; it's not about price for them, it's the illusion of price."

Stu could feel his own anger starting to rise. *Charlie has been in this business long enough to know better than to make it about price; we both know that.*

"That's just the point, Charlie; it's *not* about price half the time. And even when it is, you have to be able to sell the illusion that it isn't. You've got to convince your clients that we're doing this for them, that it's to their advantage, that we want to save them the hassle of bargaining and negotiating. I mean, Charlie, if you can't sell that, I don't know what to tell you."

Charlie sighed and looked away. "I don't know, either, Stu. I guess we both have some decisions to make, don't we?"

"How's that?" Stu asked.

Charlie wiped his mouth off, then tossed his napkin down onto his plate. He pulled himself out of the booth. "Well," he said, as he picked up the bill, "you need to decide if you and Carl are finally going to deal with my concerns. And I need to decide if I'm going to still be working for DynaCorp next time you ask me to lunch."

Stu stood and put his hand on Charlie's shoulder. "Charlie, please . . . let's talk about this." He gently motioned for Charlie to sit down.

Charlie remained standing. "I'm serious, you know."

"I am too. I'm serious about taking your concerns back to corporate and doing more to make you happy with DynaCorp."

Charlie frowned in a moment of stunned silence. "Really?" he asked.

Stu looked him directly in the eye. "If this issue has meant this much to you, for this long, then the least I can do is sit down with Carl and share your side of the story." *I never thought I'd hear myself say that . . . I'm swallowing my pride with this one.*

"Thanks, Stu," Charlie said, "I appreciate that." He returned to his seat and the conversation started anew.

"I'm curious about something," Stu said. "When you reported to Carl, what did he think about this issue?"

"To be honest, it didn't come up then," Charlie explained. "I've only been working at DynaCorp for the past four years, and I've only had two bosses—you and Carl. When I started working here, I didn't know which way was up for the first six months; the culture was so different from what I was used to. And by the time I did have things figured out, Carl was planning his transition to VP."

"I see," said Stu, remembering to repeat back his understanding in his own words. "So you and Carl never had a conversation about using pricing in client negotiations?"

"That's right," confirmed Charlie. "And about the time I began reporting to you is when the competition started moving in."

"You mean Kelly and Pulse?" Stu asked, immediately thinking of DynaCorp's two biggest competitors.

"No . . . not just them," Charlie scoffed. "Kelly and Pulse have *always* been our competitors. I'm talking about these little satellite specialty plants that just opened up. You've heard about them, haven't you?"

Stu frowned. "I have, but refresh my memory."

Charlie continued. "One of them is called Phelan McElrath and the other one is Poly-Tastics. They are only in my territory and they serve only local area clients. They charge more for the customization, but they save money on labor and transportation. They may not have taken too much business away from us—at least, not yet, anyway. But they have figured out how to undercut us . . . and they're growing."

"I have heard about them," Stu said, "but I didn't know they were taking business away from us."

"Now maybe you understand what I'm up against."

Stu nodded. "I have another question for you."

"Shoot," Charlie said.

"A moment ago you made it sound like you were unhappy with DynaCorp. Can you tell me more about that?"

"It's not about DynaCorp," Charlie started, looking down at the table. "It's more about the satisfaction I'm getting . . . or not getting."

Stu stared at him, patiently waiting to hear more.

As Charlie continued, he showed a side of himself that Stu rarely saw.

"You have to understand; sales is in my blood. I do think we have a great product, but I've sold all kinds of different products. What I really live for is the negotia-tion—you know, the back and forth, playing the game, and closing the sale. To get the satisfaction, I've gotta have the freedom to put together a deal. I don't want to be an order-taker, and I don't want to lead a team of order takers."

Stu saw a spark in Charlie's eyes and heard the passion in his voice. *This Charlie is totally different from the guy who is complaining all the time.*

"I totally understand," Stu said. "Thanks, this will help me when I talk to Carl."

"I hope this has made a difference . . . for both our sakes," Charlie said. He checked his watch. "Oh . . . looks like it's time for us to go," he said, picking up the bill and pulling out his wallet.

Stu snatched the bill from Charlie's hand. "This one is on me."

"Well, if I had known you were picking up the tab, I would have had another dessert."

They said their goodbyes and Charlie shuffled out the door, wearing an expression of someone who was fully satisfied.

Stu sat back down to nibble on an almond cookie as the late-lunch crowd continued to dwindle. *In spite of a few bumps in the road there, this was a pretty good meeting with Charlie.*

Even without looking at the SIER* card every few moments, he'd remembered to do things like encourage the speaker to speak, clarify understanding, and take the time to discern. So he was surprised when he went to fill out his daily listening scorecard and it *still* showed quite a number of violations.

Stu sighed and began packing up his bag. *Glad my next meeting with Alfred is only a few days away. Maybe then I can get some guidance about what, exactly, I'm doing wrong.*

Build a Solid Foundation

Daily Listening Scorecard

Throughout the day, record the number of times you violate SIER*
by engaging in the following behaviors.

Number of
Instances

SENSE

1. Stopped making eye contact with the speaker _____

2. Asked someone to repeat himself/ herself because I was not focusing _____

INTERPRET

3. Misunderstood the meaning of someone's message *2*

4. Let my mind wander while someone was speaking _____

EVALUATE

5. Jumped to a conclusion about what someone was going to say *3*

6. Let my personal judgments crowd out the speaker's message _____

RESPOND

7. Interrupted someone or changed the subject in the middle of the conversation *6*

8. Reacted emotionally to what someone was saying before they finished *4*

MEMORY

9. Forgot important information (such as a person's name) while communicating with someone _____

©2012, Dr. Rick Bommelje   **LISTENING AID #2A**

CHAPTER 11
Relationships Matter

Stu was eager to share his progress with Alfred, which made it difficult for him to be patient until his next Monday morning appointment.

Even so, he decided to make the most of his weekly Sunday ritual with Jennifer—their weekly date. Today they had planned an afternoon movie followed by a long walk and end-of-day dinner at their favorite waterfront restaurant.

They giggled through the movie, quite unintentionally. It was supposed to be a serious drama, but the acting was so over-the-top, it was impossible for them to not laugh. There wasn't much to discuss on their walk afterward, except for maybe how silly the movie was.

When they were halfway to the marina Jennifer asked, "How's work, honey?"

Stu sighed heavily and said, "Well . . . it's work."

"Come on, Stu," she urged, nudging him playfully with her shoulder. An afternoon breeze pulled at the long, dark hair on either side of her face. "Don't give me an easy answer. I really want to know."

He shrugged and continued to tell her just enough. He described Rachel and her complaints, the daily grind of DynaCorp, and the pressures of industry competition. But he said nothing about Carl and the ultimatum that Stu become a better listener.

He felt torn about what he should and shouldn't share with his wife. He knew that Alfred would have encouraged him to be completely honest. But at the same time, there was a part of him that held onto a traditional—some might say antiquated—idea about what it meant to be "a man." He knew that it was old fashioned, but Stu still believed that he not only needed to provide for his wife, he also needed to protect her, shield her from some of the more unpleasant sides of his job. *She doesn't need to know about Carl's demands or my relationships with my troubled sales managers; not yet, anyway.*

"Enough about me," Stu said. They were seated at their favorite waterfront table and had ordered their first glass of wine. "How are things at school?"

Jennifer gave him a look of surprise. Stu immediately felt bad, realizing that he asked the question so rarely that Jennifer was shocked when he finally *did*. On the previous occasions when he had asked Jennifer about her work, he had used the time to "zone out" for ten or fifteen minutes while she talked about the seemingly inconsequential aspects of being an assistant principal at a private elementary school.

But today Stu heard Alfred's voice in his head, urging him on, encouraging him to use SIER* with everyone, especially his wife. He hadn't brought the card with him, but Stu purposefully ran down the list of letters in his mind. *"S" stands for Sense, "I" stands for Interpret, "E" stands for Evaluate, and "R" stands for Respond . . . and the asterisk reminds you to commit what you hear to memory.*

So far, Stu had really only used SIER* in work mode; now he was ready to give it a try in his personal life as well.

"Well, I got the nicest call today from one of the students' mothers," Jennifer began with a hopeful smile. "You know that story I told you about Bobby and the school uniform?"

"No," Stu said. "Tell me about it."

Jennifer took a long deep sigh as her eyes narrowed reproachfully. "I did tell you about it. Don't you remember?"

"Um . . . no," Stu said, reluctantly. He reminded himself that he wanted to use the skills honestly—even when it wasn't easy. "I'm sorry. When was this?"

"Two weeks ago," she said, avoiding his eyes. The expression on her face was partly surprised, but mostly resigned.

For Stu, there was no mistaking what her response meant. *I've seen this look before, but now I'm also seeing it in a new way. For her, this is just one more example of me not hearing—me not listening.*

He shook his head and looked her directly in the eye. "I'm sorry."

She shrugged and said, "That's okay."

Stu didn't need to be an expert in listening to interpret what that meant: *It wasn't really "okay." This kind of thing was never okay.*

There was an awkward silence while Stu worked to evaluate what Jennifer had just said; she was upset, clearly, but he hoped she really *did* understand that he was making an effort. Before she could say another word he added, "I'm listening now, babe."

"I'm glad," she said. He could tell she was still troubled, but a moment later she smiled all the way until her eyes crinkled.

"Please . . . I really do want to hear about it," he said.

"Well . . . you know that we have a dress code at school," Jennifer began tentatively. Since she could see that Stu was actually paying attention for a change, her effort began picking up momentum.

"About two weeks ago, I had a teacher tell me, 'Mrs. Preston, you need to talk to Bobby because he refuses to wear the uniform.' So I brought Bobby into my office and sat him down. And this little fifth-grade kid defiantly says to me, 'I don't have to wear the uniform. You can't make me wear the uniform. I won't wear the uniform.'

"The thing is, the whole time he was speaking, he was looking down at the floor. He never once looked at me directly. So I was getting some mixed messages, and I thought, 'There's something else going on here.' So I said, 'Let's call your mom and see what she says about this.' I could tell that he didn't like that idea, but he didn't say anything.

"When I looked in his records, I noticed his mother was a single mom who worked at a local restaurant. And this restaurant . . . well, let's just say that the customers there are *not* going to be big tippers. When I got to thinking about how much money his mother probably earns, and how much time she has during her week to do laundry, it just clicked.

"I decided not to call his mom. Instead, I knelt down and looked him right in the eye, and then as gently as I could, I said, 'Do you run out of clean uniforms at the end of the week?' His tough guy act just melted. His eyes welled up with tears, and he said: 'Yes, ma'am.'

"All of a sudden, it made sense. They didn't have money for trips to the laundromat, and he hadn't been wearing his uniform because it was dirty. His first response when I asked him about it was to get defensive.

"So I said, 'You know what? We can fix that. We will get you another shirt, and we have some loaner khaki pants.' Well, his face it up, and I swear he was happy as he could be. While he was in my office, I also noticed the soles of his shoes had separated from the tops. So later that day, I went out and bought him a new pair of shoes.

"Well, of course, when Margaret, my principal, found out about what I had done with Bobby—and that I had spent my own money to get him shoes—she said, 'You know, Jennifer, you can't be doing that. You don't want to get too close to these kids who are only here because they're getting a state grant. I hope he's not this much trouble moving forward.'"

Stu sat back, realizing he'd been on the edge of his seat ever since Jennifer started talking. He'd been meaning to follow SIER* but, instead, he simply followed his wife's passionate story line. He fully *sensed* the animated look on Jennifer's face and her caring tone of voice.

"So, how did everything turn out?" he pressed, as the waiter delivered their appetizer.

She let loose with a little smile and said, "Well, that's why I brought it up. I got the nicest call today from Bobby's mother, saying how much she appreciated the extra uniform and the new shoes. She was so grateful."

Stu could tell there was more to the story. He waited patiently and continued making eye contact with Jennifer.

"But . . . well, let's just say that there's a bit of tension between me and Margaret as a result of what she said about Bobby. I mean, can you imagine? This woman runs a school and she's telling me not to get 'too involved'? Suggesting that Bobby is 'trouble' because he's embarrassed to wear a dirty uniform? I just . . . I don't get it."

Stu didn't leave it at that; he pressed on and asked Jennifer some questions. *Why does Margaret feel this way? What is the school's policy?*

Eventually, Jennifer revealed that her principal was, in fact, *very* upset with her.

"She believes I crossed the line," Jennifer finally confessed. "Policy or no policy, I know in my heart that I did the right thing. Maybe for her it's a 'boss thing' to not feel compassionate at work!"

Jennifer smiled at Stu to show she meant no offense.

Stu realized, perhaps for the first time, that bosses were the same everywhere; politics, policies, and procedures often meant more than performance, personality or, for that matter, even a passion for the job. As long as he'd known Jennifer, she'd been truly passionate about kids. She didn't work just to earn a paycheck. She worked because she wanted to, because she loved kids; loved being around them and helping them grow.

Stu saw that Jennifer had broken the school's policy of not giving students special treatment. But he also saw the empathy Jennifer had for a kid who was going through a challenging situation. *What kind of principal would rather see a kid be singled out for being unkempt than have a policy broken?*

Stu found himself suddenly drawn into Jennifer's problem and seeing things from her point of view. While he was strongly tempted to offer his own reasonable solutions, he held off and let her talk. The conversation eventually turned to other topics, and continued through a bottle of wine, the entrée, and well into dessert.

They left the restaurant later than usual. As they walked through the cool darkness back to their car, Stu noted that the parking lot that had been so crowded earlier was now almost deserted. They drove home quietly, all talked out.

As the garage door closed behind them, Stu pulled the car key out of the ignition. Before he could open the driver-side door, Jennifer impulsively grabbed Stu by the hand. Surprised, he turned to look at her. There was a moment of silence—then Jennifer leaned in to give Stu a warm kiss.

"What was that for?" he asked curiously.

"Just . . . for listening to me tonight. I guess I didn't realize how much I needed to vent."

He looked at her pointedly and said, "I guess you've been needing to vent for quite a while . . . and I'm sorry if I haven't always been receptive. I'm going to work on that."

Her eyes searched his; it was clear she had never heard her husband speak like this before.

He continued. "It's not always easy for me, but I'd like to think that whenever you come to me, I will always be ready to listen."

CHAPTER 12
Develop Healthy Habits

It was early the next morning when Stu pulled into the DynaCorp headquarters parking garage. He drove all the way up to the sixth level where few cars ever ventured. The gleaming white D'Amato Detailing van was there and waiting for him.

"Morning, Alfred," Stu said, shaking the man's firm grip energetically.

"Hello, Stu," Alfred replied, quickly getting out his cleaning materials and getting to work.

Stu felt bad about this arrangement—that the teacher worked while the pupil just stood around leaning against the nearest guardrail. But Alfred seemed happy to take care of the car at the same time that he conducted the lesson in listening.

"How did things go this week?"

"Pretty good, if I do say so myself."

"Glad to hear it."

"Jennifer has really noticed a change in the way we communicate . . . and I have, too. She's really happy." As he said it, Stu felt a blush fall across his face. He was embarrassed to think that he sounded like a teenage boy with his first girlfriend.

"That's the whole point," said Alfred as he carefully polished the dashboard. "So far you've been listening like it's a chore, but eventually it will become a natural habit. That's why SIER* is so critical. By following each of the stages in order, you're committing your conversations to memory. I'm sure your wife is happier. Aren't you?"

Stu didn't have to think too hard about the question; of course he was. He gave Alfred a glance and a nod.

"So what's on the agenda for this week, Alfred?" Stu asked.

Alfred pulled another folder from the back of the van and started rifling through it. "Habits," he said. "Listening habits can make you or break you, and there are several positive habits that can consistently pay off for you."

"I'm ready," Stu declared.

Alfred invited Stu to sit, and then handed him Listening Aid 3A, the Listening Habits Profile.

Stu skimmed the profile with a willing curiosity. Then he turned to Alfred. "So ... how does it work?"

"This profile will give you some very important information about your listening habits. First, you answer these five questions; it should only take a minute or two. Read each question and select how often you engage in each habit. Don't get stalled on thinking about specific situations. Your first response is your most accurate. . . ."

Develop Healthy Habits

Listening Habits Profile

Respond to the following questions to measure how often you engage in each habit.

	Almost Always	Usually	Sometimes	Seldom	Almost Never	Score
1. How often do you find the speaker uninteresting?	❑	❑	❑	❑	❑	_____
2. How often do you criticize the speaker's speaking skills (in your mind)?	❑	❑	❑	❑	❑	_____
3. How often do you listen only for facts?	❑	❑	❑	❑	❑	_____
4. How often do you find yourself not taking notes?	❑	❑	❑	❑	❑	_____
5. How often do you fake attention to the speaker?	❑	❑	❑	❑	❑	_____

TOTAL SCORE _____

LISTENING AID #3A

Alfred's voice trailed off. Stu looked more closely at the profile, then began digging in to record his answers.

When he was done, Alfred had him turn the listening aid over, and told him how to score the profile. "For every 'Almost Always' you checked, score one point. For every 'Usually,' score two points. 'Sometimes' scores three points; 'Seldom' scores four; and every 'Never' you checked scores five points. Then add up the five items for a total score."

Stu totaled his five item scores and put a "13" in the box marked *Total*.

"What does this score mean?" he asked, showing it to Alfred.

"Let's find out, Stu. Here are the score ranges." Alfred referred to Listening Aid 3B again, and pointed to the five categories of scores.

Stu saw that his score fell squarely in the "Poor listening habits" category. "Wow ... I knew I was bad, but I didn't think I was *this* bad," Stu said.

"This isn't a 'pass' or 'fail' test," Alfred explained, using his typically gentle and understanding tone. His eyes showed that he didn't just understand Stu's plight, but genuinely wanted to help him overcome his status of "poor listening habits."

"And there's no good or bad here, either. All we're trying to do is to help you find out where you are on the listening habits scale, so we can help you get you to where you really need to be. It's just a little reminder of what you're doing and not doing. But I know that sometimes,

Develop Healthy Habits

Listening Habits Profile

Scoring

1. *Review your profile responses and use the scoring column on the right to assign a value to each of them.*

2. *Add up your scores from all five items to determine how healthy your listening habits are.*

Interpreting Your Score

23 - 25	Great listening habits
20 - 22	Very good listening habits
17 - 19	Good listening habits
14 - 16	Fair listening habits
Less than 14	Poor listening habits

©2012, Dr. Rick Bommelje   **LISTENING AID #3B**

seeing the facts in black and white can be a little . . . overwhelming."

"I'll say," Stu sighed. He smiled at Alfred good-naturedly, though inside he was actually quite disappointed. After all, he had thought he was doing quite well in the past few weeks, reaching out to his sales managers, taking time to really listen to Jennifer. The profile made him think he was not making progress. *At this rate, I'll never get to the level Carl wants me to be in six months.*

"Are you feeling a little down?" Alfred asked. As usual, his expression and the tone of his voice indicated that he already knew the answer.

"You could say that," Stu blurted.

"I hope you're not too upset with your score . . . that's not the kind of response I would want you to have. Instead, it should give you some relief to know that you have a system to help you reach your goal of being a great listener."

"I thought I was already on my way," Stu said.

"But you are!" Alfred put his hand on Stu's shoulder to reassure him. "Listening is a habit to practice, not a destination to get to. It's like any other habit: if you don't have it already, you have to acquire it. How do you do that? Practice, practice, practice!"

"Okay," said Stu. He was trying hard not to feel over-whelmed. "But I thought listening was a behavior, not a habit."

Alfred beamed. "That's a good point. In fact, it's both. *Habits* are *behaviors* that are created through constant repetition. What you've already begun doing—both at work and at home—those are behaviors that you can reinforce through repetition. The goal isn't to do them once and then forget them; that's not great listening.

Great listening means that you keep your consciousness in a place where what the other person is saying is important to you. For most of us, that requires some work.

Dr. Grove said there are five healthy habits that great listeners consistently practice. Let's take a quick look at each of them."

Alfred pulled out Listening Aid 4, labeled "Healthy Listening Habits," and passed the card to Stu.

"The first healthy habit is to *find something of interest*. In this habit, you continuously go after the point of the communication, no matter where you are or who you are with. Don't wait and let the value come to you; take the lead and go after it. Too many people simply wait for the value point to jump into their arms, only to miss it completely. You wouldn't wait for a fish to jump into your boat, would you? No . . . you'd toss out a line and actively fish for it. The same goes for seeking out those value points in *every* conversation.

"Listening becomes a tool to bridge the gap with people who see the world differently from how you do, who come from different backgrounds, and who have experienced different things. If you are going to be successful, you must become a *continuous learner*. One of the very best ways to do this is to listen for the interest or usefulness of what is being communicated. This is

Develop Healthy Habits

Healthy Listening Habits

- Find something of interest.

- Concentrate on content first, delivery second.

- Focus on the main point.

- Take notes.

- Pay genuine attention.

©2012, Dr. Rick Bommelje

LISTENING AID #4

especially true at work. Listening to the people you're working with is one of the best ways to continue to remind yourself of where they are coming from. When you take the time to understand someone else's point of view, you will do a better job of positioning your ideas so they can buy into them."

Stu wanted to show Alfred he was following along. "I can see the value of being a continuous learner. You have to do that if you want to succeed in business."

"I'm glad you get that. As I said before, listening isn't a one-time event. Rather, it's a lifelong process, and we're always learning. Now, are you ready for the next habit?"

"Do I have a choice?" Stu gulped.

"Not today!" Alfred laughed. "The second healthy habit is to *concentrate on content first, delivery second*. In other words, people are sending you messages all of the time and it is important to remember that, as the listener, *content is king*.

"Too often we expect certain messages to be delivered in a particular kind of way. If we are anticipating bad news or a reprimand, then we expect the speaker to be yelling. If someone is speaking softly, then we think maybe their message isn't as important. The fact is, there are as many different communication styles as there are people communicating. So it's important to concentrate on the content first, the delivery second.

"What I'm saying is that the message may not come in the exact package you want it delivered in. The speaker may talk in a monotone, or have an accent that is difficult to understand, or she may wear her hair in some odd way.

But that doesn't mean that what's being said isn't important. These are all just part of the delivery; they should have no effect on your perception of what is actually being said. The content should take first place, and the delivery second."

"I can see the value in that," Stu said, nodding his head. "I think sometimes I don't pay attention to what people are saying because of how they say it. They are trying to make a point, but I get distracted by some piece of their delivery. They can tell I'm distracted, it makes them angry, and then they have to start screaming at me. At that point, they've got my attention, but again, for the wrong reasons."

"Screaming is a very ineffective way of communication. If it gets to that point, you're right, real communication is often lost. That's why these are such great habits to acquire; the sooner you do them, the sooner everyone around you becomes a better communicator. Are you ready for the next one?"

"Let's press on," Stu said with confidence.

"The third healthy habit is to *focus on the main point,* rather than on the many facts imbedded in a message. Many people, when communicating, think that more is better. They think that if they simply 'talk around' the issue with more words, it will distract attention away from the fact that they don't really know what they're talking about. This is especially true at work. As a habitual listener, you must become—"

"Like a sponge?" Stu interrupted. He was eager to interject something into the conversation.

But Alfred smiled and shook his head. "Not quite, but you're getting the idea. A sponge will soak up anything: water, juice, milk, grease, it doesn't matter. What you want to be is more like . . . *a filter.* When people are throwing everything at you, fact after fact, word after word, you want to pick and choose which words matter the most, not just anything."

Stu grumbled good-naturedly. He decided to do a better job of holding his tongue from now on.

"The reason you want to be a filter," Alfred continued, "is that you can remember more facts if you focus on the main idea rather than try to memorize all the facts that are coming at you at once. It's like juggling: if you aren't very good, you will most likely drop some balls. And the more balls you try to keep in the air, the more you're likely to drop.

"The same thing is true when trying to memorize points of information. As you juggle the many points as they come at you, sooner or later you will miss some and drop others. But if you ignore, or at least filter out, the less important points—or maybe I should say the less *relevant* points—you're more likely to grasp the bigger picture the person is trying to communicate to you. Simply put, get the main point and the supporting points will follow.

"The fourth healthy habit is to *take notes.* This is one of my favorites. The notes can be written *or* mental. There are many different types of note-taking systems, but the key is that you are in a better position to know things if you 'note' them first."

Stu jumped in with a concern. "That seems like a waste of time. I don't see how paper note taking would work in a conversation."

"Why not?" Alfred countered. "When you're at a restaurant, haven't you ever seen a waitress write down your order as you give it to her?"

"Yeah, but... it always impresses me more if she doesn't have to write it down."

Alfred nodded thoughtfully. Then he replied, "What impresses you more? If the waitress writes down your order and brings everything you asked for, or if she doesn't write it down and completely screws it up?"

Stu frowned. "I suppose you have a point, but I'd prefer to take notes in my head."

"Many people do; whatever works for you is what's going to work in the end. The fact remains, you're not going to do something—habitually, I mean—if it's physically uncomfortable for you to do it. So if it feels unnatural for you to physically take notes, then take them mentally. I'm just saying you'll want to create some kind of system, so it feels natural for you to mentally take notes as someone's speaking. But recognize that learning means that sometimes you need to take yourself into your 'discomfort zone.' With this in mind, I would challenge you to take written notes, too."

Stu nodded, picturing how intense that might be. "I suppose I could always try both and see which one works best."

"Now you're talking." Alfred beamed. He continued, "The fifth healthy habit is to *pay genuine attention*. This may sound simple, but it requires a great deal of energy to be fully and *genuinely* in the moment with someone. The payoff is that they actually will be able to feel it when you are paying genuine attention.

"There's an old saying that goes 'wherever you are, *be there.*' This means that even if you'd rather be anywhere else, at home or a movie or the ballpark or the beach, it doesn't matter; *be where you are.* You're already there, right? So . . . why not physically and mentally be in that moment until the moment's over? This habit alone can substantially increase your listening potential.

"Paying genuine attention will also help you avoid becoming distracted," Alfred continued. "We live in a fast-paced and noisy world, and that makes it especially hard on even the best listeners out there. There are all kinds of noises and distractions—both external and internal. We will cover this later when we get to the strategy of 'Ditch the Distractions.'

"Speaking of distractions," Alfred said, "one of the reasons it takes significant effort to avoid them is the fact that you can process hundreds of words a minute and the average person speaks at the rate of only 130 to 170 words a minute. You can take in four to seven times that number of words in your mind; so this means that you can process over 500 words a minute."

"How do I stay with the speaker if I have this much capacity?" Stu asked.

"One way to stay with them is to practice the PTRB method. PTRB stands for *plan to report back.* During every communication that you have, be able to report back the main point of the message. This will keep you focused and 'in the game.'"

Alfred finally wound down his message as he recited from memory the five healthy listening habits.

"Wow, Alfred . . . I have to be honest, that seems like a lot of work!"

"I know it does . . . right now." Alfred laughed good-naturedly. He went on to explain, "Dr. Grove used to tell us that learning to listen was like building up a muscle. You won't get any stronger if you don't work it!"

Alfred pointed again to the listening aid that showed the healthy listening habits. "So, as we close out our lesson on the strategy of developing healthy habits, your assignment for our next session is to identify at least two habits that you believe you should work on immediately and bring back specific examples of how you have put them into action. You think you can do that?"

Stu nodded, wondering which of the habits he might choose to focus on.

CHAPTER 13
Restarting

Even though Stu had walked past the door to the IT department hundreds of times, this was the first time he had ever gone inside. As his eyes adjusted to the darkness, he saw that the receptionist's desk was completely empty—no computer, phone, office supplies, or receptionist; apparently someone had decided that greeting people was not important. The waiting area was meager: two office chairs and a small table. There, Stu found Rachel checking emails on her laptop. They greeted each other with a tense formality.

"Thanks for coming all the way to headquarters for this meeting," he said.

"If that's what it takes . . . " she replied.

They both sat, stiffly, avoiding eye contact, as they waited for the others to arrive.

"Great weather we're having, isn't it?" Stu said, trying to engage her.

"You'd never know it in here," Rachel replied, leaning over to look down a dimly lit corridor of cubicles. "No windows, no daylight . . . I wouldn't want to work in a place like this."

"I think they spend most of their time in the field," he said.

A quiet moment passed.

Suddenly, the door opened. The glare streaming in from the hallway made it hard for Stu and Rachel to make sense of what they were seeing. When the door closed, it became clear that two men had entered the room. One was dressed in professional attire; the other wore khaki pants and a loose-fitting corporate-logo shirt.

"Are you Stu and Rachel?" asked the man wearing the tie.

They squinted and nodded in the affirmative.

"Sorry to keep you waiting. I'm Jeff Andrews, the director of IT . . . and this is Roger Logan, one of our technicians. Roger's going to be helping us today."

They all shook hands. Stu and Rachel followed as the two men led them to the end of the shadowy corridor to a dead-end set of unoccupied cubicles. The director pulled out four chairs and arranged them to face each other in the middle of the alleyway. He turned on some desk lamps so they could see each other. "Sorry we don't have a conference room to meet in," he said.

Rachel rolled her eyes.

"That's okay," Stu said. "We're just glad you have some time for us."

Jeff initiated the discussion. "So, let's get started. There's a problem with some software?"

Stu invited Rachel to describe the situation. Over the course of the next twenty minutes, she detailed the challenges her team had in using the software, how the reporting features were not accurate, and how this was affecting her operation. Jeff actively engaged her by asking questions, trying to understand her complaints.

As Stu listened, he reminded himself that this was an opportunity to practice the second healthy habit: Concentrate on content first, delivery second. *I've heard her tell this story many times, and I find her smug delivery irritating. I'm going to try and overlook her attitude and focus on her message.*

He focused his attention on the content by practicing another healthy habit: taking notes in a small spiral-bound notebook. Stu noticed that Jeff's questions were rather general and high-level in nature; instead of trying to understand the software and its problems, he seemed more focused on how the salespeople used it. Stu also noticed that the technician, Roger, sat silently, looking bored and irritated. Remembering that the first healthy habit was to find something of interest, it was clear to Stu that Roger could not be more disinterested. On one occasion, the technician quietly yawned. *I would feel the same way. Jeff and Rachel seem to be talking around the problem . . .*

Stu waited for a break in the conversation. When the opportunity presented itself, he interjected. "Roger, do you have any questions?"

Both Rachel and Jeff looked up, as if they had just noticed Roger's presence for the first time.

The technician hesitated, but Stu persisted. "Please, I'd like to hear what you think."

"Well, since you asked . . . I'm not a salesperson and this is kind of hard for me to follow. Shouldn't we just open it up and take a look at it?"

They all glanced at each other, but Stu responded first. "That sounds like a good idea," he said. "It would be helpful to see what Rachel's talking about."

They adjusted their chairs around one cubicle and turned on the computer. The desktop monitor was large enough for all four of them to huddle around. Rachel, sitting at the keyboard, logged in to the software and proceeded directly to the list of invoices for her branch. Prepared to make her case, she reached into her bag and pulled out a hand-held calculator. "Stu, could you help with this?" she asked.

Stu took the calculator and followed her instructions. Carefully, Rachel went line by line through her quarterly revenues, calling out figures for Stu to enter. When she got to the bottom, she said to Stu, "Hit total."

Stu did so and held up the calculator for her to see, as he declared the quarterly sales figure for Rachel's branch.

"Now watch this," she said. Rachel proceeded to the analysis tab to run the report. A moment later, she called out the total figure that appeared on the monitor—an amount that was significantly lower than what had been added up on the calculator. Stu quickly did the math. There was a discrepancy of about 4 percent.

"Wow," Stu said. "Rachel, you were right." He scribbled the figures into his notebook.

"*Now* I'm right, huh?" Rachel glared at him. "I told you so! I've been saying this for months now, and you kept treating me like I was making it up!"

Stu felt some discomfort at being called out in such a way in front of two corporate colleagues. But he remembered his focus on the healthy habits; he was determined not to react to her. He smiled weakly at Jeff and Roger, who seemed to take the whole thing in stride.

"So, guys . . . you see what we're talking about here. Any explanation?" Stu asked.

Roger and Jeff exchanged glances.

"I'm going to defer to the technician on this one," Jeff said diplomatically.

Slowly, Roger opened up to share what was on his mind. His demeanor and delivery were quiet and measured. "I've been hearing rumors about the new version of this software from several different branches," he said. "But you are the first ones who made an effort to show us."

"I knew it!" Rachel said. "So the other branches are having the same kind of trouble?"

"Some of them are," Roger replied. "But only two regions were selected to roll out the software as 'early adopters.' The rest of the company is still using the old version."

"So what are you saying?" Rachel asked impatiently.

"Well, I'm not completely sure, but I have a theory about why your numbers might appear to be underreported. And let's just say that I have some good news, and some bad news."

Rachel rolled her eyes again. Stu nodded at Roger to carry on, all the while continuing to capture his notes.

"The good news is that I clearly see how much more complicated the new version of the software is."

"Yes!" Rachel said. "The way the screens are organized is confusing, and it takes longer to input data."

"Yeah," Roger agreed. "It's definitely not user friendly."

"Right," Rachel said. "So what's the bad news?"

"The bad news," Roger paused carefully to formulate his words, "is that it doesn't *really* have any glitches that cause underreporting. I think the real problem is user error."

Rachel looked over at Stu, then back at Roger. She pursed her lips and took a deep breath. "Based on what?" she asked.

"Well, let me show you." Roger took a seat at the keyboard. Maneuvering the mouse around the software screens, he explained his assumptions. "The new version of the software is designed to import information from the old version of the software. But at the same time, we ask the sales reps to update information about each client. It feels like there's a lot of stuff in here to fill out for each client and each contract—tax rates, discounts, commission rates. It's all really confusing. Some sales reps check the information to make sure it's accurate; some don't."

Roger maneuvered to a set of screens that Stu had never seen before. He could tell from Rachel's expression that she had never seen them either.

"There is a bit of a bug between the old version and the new version when the data is imported," Roger explained. "For some reason, the commissions and the discount rates get factored into a client formula before the data comes over. Then the sales reps may put in new information on top of that, which causes some accounts to get double discounts or double commissions. But it doesn't tell you that unless you have a certain window selection turned on. It just shows up in the report. It all depends on whether the sales reps thoroughly check their data or not."

Roger quietly stood up and stepped away from the computer. "So . . . I think that's why your numbers might be lower than they ought to be."

Stu was suitably impressed with Roger's logic. *He certainly didn't have to yell and scream to make his point.*

"Rachel, do you have any questions?" Stu asked.

She shook her head; still speechless, she was processing all that she had heard.

"So what solution do you recommend?" Stu asked.

Roger and Jeff exchanged glances.

"Again, I'm going to defer to the technician," Jeff smiled.

Roger responded. "I'd like to spend some time with it and make sure my theory is correct. Maybe by next week, I'll know."

"And if it turns out your theory is correct?" Stu asked.

"Some software training for the sales reps probably wouldn't hurt," Roger said.

"Software *re-training*," Rachel said, under her breath.

They spent a few more minutes discussing the matter, exploring options for moving forward and how they could help each other. Then, Stu and Rachel thanked them for their time and made their way back to the sunlit hallway. The moment they came through the door, Rachel was all business, sliding her laptop bag onto her shoulder and striding quickly down the hallway.

After jogging a few steps to catch up to her pace, Stu called out to her. "Rachel?"

She stopped mid-stride and turned to face him.

"Could you spare a few minutes?" he asked.

"What for?" Rachel asked with a resigned face.

"Nothing in particular." He pointed down the hallway toward the company cafeteria. "I was just thinking . . . we could have a cup of coffee before you head out."

She tilted her head at him and huffed. "Okay . . . make it a cup of tea and you've got a deal."

Her pace became more leisurely as they walked side by side toward the cafeteria. As they pushed through the double doors, they saw that the lunchtime crowd had subsided, and they found a comfortable table by the windows.

"It feels good to be back in the daylight again," he said.

She gave a slight smile. "It does,'" she agreed. Taking a sip of tea, she seemed to relax.

While Stu waited for his tea to cool, he took out his notepad to summarize what he had written down during the meeting.

"Are you a detective now?" Rachel smirked.

Stu paused, not certain of how to interpret her question. "How do you mean?" he asked.

"Well, you know how the detectives on those old TV shows would scribble in their little notebooks? That's what you're reminding me of today."

"Oh," Stu laughed softly. His face conveyed a bit of embarrassment as he confessed, "Actually . . . I'm working on my listening. The notes help me."

Rachel responded in her usual snarky tone. "So *that's* where all this is coming from. You're actually paying attention."

Stu quickly responded. "I've *always* paid attention to you, Rachel; I just thought you were . . . um . . . overstating those reporting problems."

Rachel's eyes widened; she was ready to launch into defense mode again.

Stu held his hand up to reassure her. "Now I see that you were right . . . and I was wrong."

His comment appeased her. "Is that an apology?" she asked.

"I suppose it is, yes," Stu said. Thoughtfully, he added, "I do want to acknowledge something. A few weeks ago, when we had our field meeting, you challenged me on whether or not I had checked out the new software. The truth is . . . while I have used the software to run reports, today was the first time I saw how the new software works from the sales rep point of view. And you were right—it is overly complicated. I can see why people are having problems with it."

"Thanks," she smiled. "Well, for what it's worth, it turns out I *wasn't* right. I was so sure there was a glitch in the software. But then when he showed us those screens, and I had never seen them before. I felt so . . . wrong."

He nodded, closing the book and putting it away to give Rachel his full attention. "I know, I felt the same way," he said, hoping to make her feel better.

She paused a moment before asking, "So how do you think we should fix this?"

Stu looked up. "The software situation, you mean?"

"Yes," she said.

Stu sighed. "Well, we need to wait and see what information Roger comes back with. But if it turns out that the problem is user error, here are two things we can do. First, I can set up a meeting between you, me, Carl, and Jeff to decide if we want to go back to using the previous version, or if we want to invest in providing everyone with training to use it properly. Second, and in the meantime, I can work with you to figure out a way to determine how far your numbers are off—low, high, or in between—so we'll be able to get a more accurate picture of sales at your branch."

She smiled. "That was all I ever asked for."

Stu's face lit up with a grin, surprised at her pleasant response.

Teasing, she added, "Yeah, that was all I asked for . . . about three months ago!"

He shook his head and smiled again, recognizing a Rachel that was more true to form.

They stood and walked out together into the hall and past the reception area.

"Where are you parked today?" he asked.

"Out in front . . . I used a visitor spot," she said.

"I'll walk you there," he said. "I still need a little more sunshine."

They walked out into the pleasant crispness of a beautiful afternoon.

"You know," she said, "this meeting didn't turn out the way I expected it to. I wanted to be vindicated, and . . . I wasn't. But now that it's all done, I think we accomplished a lot."

"I do too," Stu said.

As they reached her car, Rachel turned to face him. "In the cafeteria back there you said you were wrong about me, remember?"

"I did," he admitted, holding her door open.

She slung her laptop bag onto the passenger seat. As she slid inside, she continued. "I have to admit," she said thoughtfully, "I was wrong about you, too. Thanks for a great meeting."

She closed her car door and gave him a wave as she pulled out of the parking lot.

He stood outside in front of the building for some time, the mid-afternoon sun rivaling the brightness of the smile on his face. *It's working. Whatever Alfred is doing, it's working. And what did he say last time we met? "It's not enough to know the strategies on a conceptual level; you have to practice them. Learning to listen is like building up a muscle—you won't get any stronger if you don't work it."*

Stu took a moment to pull out his notebook again. He reviewed his list of the five healthy listening habits, and his plan to work on two this week, two the next week, and then the last one, until he had them down cold.

Then he reached into his bag and slid out the "Listening Pays" card Alfred had given him. He was reminded that he and Alfred had covered only two strategies so far, and still had four more to go.

Stu turned and walked back into DynaCorp, realizing he still had a long day ahead of him and much more to learn.

LISTENING PAYS

Achieve Significance through the Power of Listening

Six Strategies

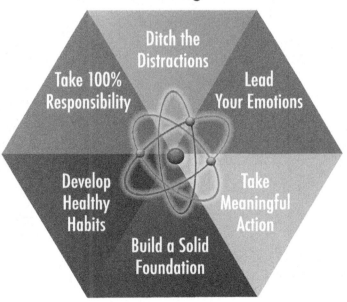

CHAPTER 14
Take 100% Responsibility

Stu pulled his car over to the side of the road while the traffic on some unnamed street whizzed by him. He tapped his mobile phone and was irritated to see that the battery had died. Embarrassed by the idea of asking strangers for directions, he leaned over and popped open the glove compartment. He pulled out the rarely-used GPS unit and plugged it in. *Amazing that it still works—glad I didn't cancel that subscription.*

He punched in his intended location—Riverview Park—and sighed impatiently as he waited for the map to appear.

Earlier that morning, when he set out on his errands, he had checked the clock. There was plenty of time before his appointment, so he stopped for coffee and got caught up on the news. Then he swung by the post office to drop off some mail. Finally on his way to the park, he checked again and saw there was still plenty of time. But he couldn't have predicted there would be an accident on

Schuyler Avenue that would back up traffic for two blocks. And in his attempt to drive around the pile-up, he couldn't have known that he would encounter road construction taking him on a detour through a new neighborhood that the GPS considered uncharted territory.

Under other circumstances, he might have treated this like an entertaining adventure; exploring unfamiliar side streets on his way to a somewhat familiar place. But he didn't have time to be an explorer today. He was running late for his scheduled appointment with Alfred. And now—as much as he didn't want to admit it—he was lost.

Stu reassured himself that it was no big deal. *Alfred won't mind my being late; besides, it's not my fault.*

But his internal reassurances weren't helping him find his destination, and neither, apparently, was the navigation device. At one intersection, the soothing electronic female voice commanded Stu to turn left . . . onto a street that flowed only to the right. Stu paused . . . noticed the one-way sign and arrows . . . saw the oncoming traffic . . . and started cursing at the machine. Having gotten some of the anger out of his system, he drove straight through the intersection, hoping to pick up a parallel street. The voice calmly informed him that she was "recalculating." Stu felt like telling the navigation voice to shut up. *Don't you understand that I'm running late because of you?*

After several more curves and corners that made him feel like he was going even farther in the wrong direction, he arrived at last at Riverview Park. He spotted the gleaming white van parked near the water fountain. And there, on a park bench beneath a towering old elm, was Alfred—seated and peacefully meditating.

As Stu approached, the older gentleman looked up, smiled, and put in his cochlear implant. "Good morning!" Alfred said, standing up and extending his hand.

"I'm so sorry I'm late," Stu said, pocketing his car keys. "There was an accident on Schuyler Avenue, and then I ran into construction. I got a little bit lost, and then my GPS made things worse, and, well . . . anyway . . . sorry about that."

"I'm not," said Alfred, as he moved to lean casually against the back of his van. "I mean, I am sorry that we won't get to spend as much time together today, but . . . I'm not sorry you were late."

Stu frowned as he inquired, "We won't get to spend as much time together?"

"Well, no . . . because of the time we lost."

"It was only twenty minutes, I mean . . . "

"*Twenty-five minutes*," Alfred pointed out neutrally.

There was a pause, and then Alfred asked, "Stu, don't you have days that are full of meetings scheduled back to back?"

"Sure I do. That's a big part of my job. Why?"

"Can you tell me what happens when one of the meetings in the morning goes longer than expected—for whatever reason—and how that affects your day?"

Stu grunted, slightly frustrated. He felt bad for being late, but he thought Alfred would understand. *Alfred knows that I have places to go and people to see, the same way that he does. It's not like I'm being compensated for spending time with him.*

Alfred was persistent. "Please . . . describe it for me."

"Well, it's kind of a pain when that happens," Stu explained bluntly. "It can really mess up the rest of the day."

Alfred remained quiet, indicating he was eager for Stu to finish.

Stu continued. "When I'm in charge of the meetings, I try to be clear how much time I have available, and that the rest of my day is contingent on sticking to that schedule. To go over that time limit would be, well . . . rude."

Alfred nodded, then shrugged. "Why do you think it's rude?"

"Because . . . it risks pushing all the meetings that follow later, and disrupting everyone else. And the only way to get things back on track is to have someone on the schedule get shortchanged."

Stu looked up to find Alfred calmly staring at him, wearing a slight smile.

"So . . . I guess you're saying that's what happened here today?" Stu asked.

Alfred responded evenly. "Well, I do have three appointments lined up after this one. Should I call all three of them and push them back because this one was late?"

Even though Stu saw the point that Alfred was trying to make, he quickly frowned. "No, of course you shouldn't.

But this is different because it wasn't my fault. I left the house with time to spare. How was I to know that I would get stuck in traffic because of an accident? Or that I would take a detour around road construction and get lost?"

Alfred got up and opened the rear door to the van, pulling out the green folder that was hanging inside. He returned to the park bench and handed the materials to Stu.

As both men held onto opposite ends of the folder, Alfred spoke with a tone of caution. "Before you look at today's material, I want you to remember what I asked you to think about last time. And that is, to take 100 percent responsibility for your actions—not just how you listen, but how you create a careful listening atmosphere. Look at you."

"What about me?" Stu asked, a slight edge to his voice.

"Look at your posture," Alfred said, finally letting go of his end of the folder. "Your body language is screaming that you're not in a 'good place' to receive today's message; and it's an important one. Your mind isn't on what I'm telling you right now; it's on how you might be the one who gets shortchanged today, or how your schedule might be as messed up as a result of being late. It looks to me like right now you're thinking about everything *but* listening."

Stu shook his head. "But you said you weren't upset that I was late."

Alfred grinned and shook his head. "You're not listening. I said I wasn't 'sorry' you were late. That's a lot different than not being upset about it. Whether or not it's considered rude, I now have to decide either to cut our session short, or to call my three appointments and tell them I'm running late."

"But I already told you, it wasn't my fault."

Alfred's thoughtful grin faltered as he sighed in disappointment. "Today we're here to talk about taking 100 percent responsibility for how you communicate . . . and yet it appears you're blaming your lateness on 'circumstances'—and you could have called me to let me know you were running late."

"I intended to call you, but . . . ," Stu started defending himself again, then abruptly stopped when he realized that his point sounded like yet another excuse. *Alfred is right; I could have been on time. What's more, I should have been on time.*

"So, what you're saying is . . . I could have used my time more wisely, planned my route to the park, asked directions instead of relying on my faulty GPS, or called you to let you know I was running late . . . and if I had arrived on time, I would be more relaxed and receptive to today's lesson. Is that it?"

Finally, Alfred's trademark smile returned. "I think you're getting it."

Stu nodded, relieved to know that he and Alfred were back on course. He already felt bad about being late; being called out on it made him feel even worse. But with that behind them, Stu was ready to take a breath and open his mind—and heart—to today's lesson. "All right, Alfred," he quipped. "I'm here, and I'm ready to use the time available as best as we can. What have you got for me?"

"Well, as I've already emphasized, the main point of our session today is for you to understand the importance of taking 100 percent responsibility when you communicate. Not ninety, not eighty-five, not seventy ... rather, the full 100 percent."

Stu nodded to show he was paying attention.

Alfred continued. "Dr. Grove said that in its simplest form, communication involves the connection between senders and receivers.

"You are constantly switching hats when you communicate. Speaker ... listener ... speaker ... listener. And it's not just once or twice in a conversation; it's hundreds if not thousands of times during every day.

"For years, Dr. Grove asked leaders around the world the simple question, 'Who holds the primary responsibility for successful communication—the sender or receiver?' Stu, who do *you* think it is? Sender or receiver?"

"That's a no brainer," Stu replied. "It's the sender. They know what they want to say." He thought a moment, and then added. "But, wait ... knowing you, and your emphasis on listening, the answer must be the listener, right?"

Alfred smiled cryptically before continuing, "On a consistent basis, Dr. Grove found that 70 percent of those asked believed the primary responsibility rested with the sender; 25 percent said the responsibility was with the receiver; and 5 percent expressed no comment. So it turns out many people place the responsibility for communication success on others."

Alfred paused, looking at Stu pointedly.

Stu felt a slight blush creep up his neck; then he offered, "Kind of like how people want to place the responsibility for being late on everything and everybody else, right?"

"That might be an appropriate example. In the end, there is only one person who can legitimately be held responsible for your successful communication: *you*. Successful communicators profit by using a workable and proven strategy: by taking 100 percent responsibility whenever they are in the role of the sender *or* the receiver. The key is to take the full and maximum responsibility as you constantly move between the roles of sender and receiver."

"But wait," Stu interrupted gently as he shifted in his seat on the park bench. "I don't really have a problem with the 'speaking' aspect. I mean, my boss, Carl, never once called me on the carpet for talking too much!"

Alfred chuckled playfully. "I suppose not!" But then he added, "Speaking is also a big part of listening. If you are the listener, it is very important to know the speaker's purpose. Likewise, when you speak, you should always know the listener's purpose. That's because communicating is about connecting, and strong connections are made when the people communicating share the same purpose."

Stu countered, "I don't quite understand. In my job in particular, as a salesperson, it's rare that I and the person

I'm speaking to—the receiver—ever share the same purpose."

"How so?" Alfred asked.

"Well, it's my job to close the sale. If the client walked into the room ready to sign a contract, then there would be no point to my job. I have to influence the client to see things in a certain way, so my way looks attractive to them. So if I do my best to communicate my message, and the client still doesn't get it, then there is something wrong with their ability to listen. And that's not my problem."

Alfred redirected Stu's interpretation. "Based on what you just said, I'd like to ask you to SIER* yourself. It sounds as if you are looking for an 'out' by blaming the listener. Whether you're speaking *or* listening, sending *or* receiving, you have 100 percent responsibility for *your* actions and the way the communication, the connection, is going. That's the whole point.

"Communication breakdowns like the ones your boss brought up generally occur when the speaker and listener communicate at cross-purposes."

"I'm not sure what you mean," Stu said honestly.

"Let's look at the next listening aid and you'll see how the purposes of communication are all laid out."

Stu opened the green folder and there, right on top, was Listening Aid 5A: The Five Purposes of Communication.

Take 100% Responsibility

Five Purposes of Communication

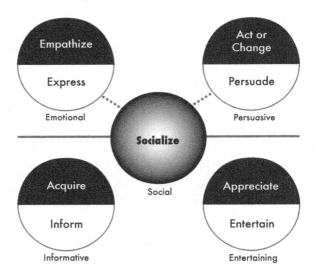

In any interaction:

- Recognize your purpose, as well as the other person's.

- Remember that socializing (a.k.a. "small talk") is the gateway to emotional connection and/or the opportunity to persuade.

LISTENING AID #5A

"There are five major purposes of communication: social, informative, persuasive, emotional, and entertaining," Alfred explained.

Stu looked carefully at the card, following along as Alfred outlined each of the points he wanted to make. "*Social* communication is the small talk of life: weather, news, sports, movies, and all kinds of everyday topics of conversation. *Informative* communication deals with facts, details, and ideas. *Persuasive* communication involves one person trying to influence someone else. In your world—the world of sales—persuasion is a critical purpose."

There was a pause as Stu looked up to acknowledge the point.

Alfred continued. "The *emotional* purpose is about sharing feelings with others, either venting as a speaker, or listening with empathy to someone who is expressing emotion. Finally, the *entertaining* purpose is speaking and listening to gain pleasure and appreciation."

"But," Stu blurted, "aren't some of these purposes, like persuasive and informative, more important than the others?"

Alfred shook his head gently. "It may appear that way at first. Take 'entertaining,' for instance. Pleasure might not be your sole purpose for communicating on the job, but think about how often your biggest sales came about because you connected with a client about something pleasurable. Think about the pleasure that comes from telling a story about fishing . . . about your favorite sports team . . . or a movie, an author, or a restaurant . . . or telling a great joke. You can never underestimate the value of any of these purposes. Remember, all communication is vital.

"The key is to match purposes with others. If you take 100 percent responsibility, either when you are speaking or listening, you will be seeking to connect with the other person's purpose."

Alfred pointed to the diagram. "I want to make this very clear for you. You'll notice in the diagram that four of the purposes are divided into two halves. That's because each person in the interaction plays a specific role.

"If your intent is to *entertain*, and the other person doesn't *appreciate* your message, then the interaction has failed as *entertaining* communication.

"If your intent is to *inform*, and the other person doesn't *acquire* your message, then the interaction has failed as *informative* communication.

"If your intent is to *express* emotion, and the other person doesn't *empathize* with your message, then the interaction has failed as *emotional* communication.

"If your intent is to *persuade*, and the other person doesn't *act or change* based on your message, then the interaction has failed as *persuasive* communication.

"So what you see here is that understanding the other person's purpose can help you understand your role in the communication. And it also shows you that both people need to play their part in order for the communication to be *purposeful*. When both people play their part well, there can be a benefit. When one person in the interaction doesn't play the part—doesn't care about the message or the other person's response—there is a cost.

"So as I mentioned before, communication breakdowns generally occur when the speaker and listener communicate at cross-purposes."

Alfred challenged Stu to apply what he was learning. "Can you think of an example in which your communication has been at cross purposes?"

Stu thought for a moment. "I suspect there have been a number of times when my wife was upset and wanted to express her emotions. But instead of empathizing with her, as she wanted me to, I chose to persuade her that her situation was not so bad. Her purpose was emotional, and mine was persuasive."

"And how did your approach make her feel?" Alfred asked.

"I would guess that she felt like I was dismissing her emotions."

"And so was either communication purpose met?"

"No . . . her emotions were not acknowledged, and I was not able to persuade her to see things differently."

"And what was the cost?"

Stu sighed and looked up at Alfred. "I get it," he said. "Each time we are at cross-purposes, it weakens the connection."

Alfred nodded and gave Stu a moment to consider how all of this applied to him.

Stu's curiosity returned. "And what about social communication? Why is that one different?"

"Social communication isn't shown as having two halves like the others, because the roles of sender-receiver switch back and forth so quickly. The intent of both parties is only to socialize."

"And what do the lines mean?"

Alfred explained, "This points out the importance of social communication. The two purposes on the bottom—informative and entertaining—can happen among people regardless of their relationships. However, the two at the top—emotional and persuasive communication—are more likely to be effective when you have a trusting relationship with the other person.

"Some people would say that social communication is a waste of time. However, social communication helps you build relationships. Therefore, it serves as a bridge to two of the other purposes—emotional and persuasive. It is very difficult to influence others without some previous relationship being built. This is why it is helpful to know a little bit about the people we interact with. It's also very unlikely that people will vent their feelings to you unless some kind of a relationship has been established. Let's look at it another way."

Alfred instructed Stu to turn the card over. On Listening Aid 5B, Stu saw the five purposes of communication laid out as an illustration of a medieval castle.

Take 100% Responsibility

Five Purposes of Communication

*If you want to be invited inside the castle,
you must engage the guard.*

LISTENING AID #5B

Alfred continued, "Stu, think of yourself and everyone around you as being like this castle. In going about your business, you meet numerous acquaintances, strangers, and other 'outsiders'—people with whom you don't have particularly strong relationships. And in general, it's easy for you to get information or entertainment from these people. Out in the world, people's agendas can be hidden or out in the open; it doesn't matter, because you don't— and can't—have relationships with everyone.

"But consider the fraction of the population that you *do* have relationships with. How do you get to know them? How do you decide whether or not you want to invite them inside your castle?"

Stu smirked at the idea, but then studied the graphic carefully. "Based on what I see here, it looks like social communication helps you decide who you want to let in, and who you want to keep out."

"That's right," Alfred said. "Social communication is the 'small talk' of life that helps you get to know people. When you take the time to become familiar with people, you uncover shared values, and build trust and rapport. You've heard the phrase 'letting your guard down,' haven't you?"

"Sure," said Stu. "We use it in sales training to describe relationship building with customers."

"Well," Alfred continued, "when you let your guard down, you are letting someone inside your castle. That means that you are ready to have an emotional connection with them, or that you trust them enough to let them persuade you—or be persuaded by you. And those people become your family, friends, and partners."

Stu looked up from the graphic and nodded his head. "I've never heard it put quite like this before, but the caption makes sense: 'If you want to be invited inside the castle, you must engage the guard.'"

"Exactly." Alfred smiled. "You can't build a relationship after just one meeting, and you can't build *trusting* relationships when your communication is at cross purposes. Social communication lets you get to know others—*and helps them get to know you*—in a way that is safe. Over time, the guard comes down so you can enjoy stronger emotional bonds, and greater influence. You become an 'insider' in somebody else's castle, and they become one in yours."

"I get it," Stu said. "But how do you make sure that you and the other person share the same purpose?"

Alfred held up his fist. "Yes, that's an important task, and one that requires patience." Then, he held up his index finger to indicate he would be right back.

Stu watched as Alfred went to his van, reached inside, and pulled something out. As he came walking back, Stu saw that he held a long, narrow stick. Tied to the stick were some feathers and beads that rattled as Alfred approached.

"Do you know what this is?" Alfred asked.

"I haven't a clue," Stu said.

Alfred explained, "For centuries, many Native American tribes have used a tool, the 'talking stick,' as they have named it, to take 100 percent responsibility. It's used to designate who has the right to speak in a gathering."

Stu jokingly asked, "They need a stick to do it? Couldn't they just take turns?"

"You would think so, but even though they didn't have boardrooms or conference calls or bonus incentives when the talking stick was first used, Native Americans took communication very seriously—between tribes, between warriors, and between themselves. The fact is, even today, when matters of great concern come before the council, the leading elder will hold the talking stick and begin the discussion.

"When he finishes what he has to say, the elder will hold out the talking stick, and whoever wishes to speak after him will take it. In this manner the stick is passed from one individual to another until all who wish to speak have done so. The stick is then passed back to the leading elder.

"The stick carries respect for free speech and assures the speaker that he has the freedom and power to say what is in his heart without fear of interruption, humiliation, or punishment.

"Whoever holds the talking stick has the sacred power of words. Only the person holding the stick can speak; the other council members have to remain silent. The eagle feather tied to the talking stick symbolizes the courage and wisdom a speaker needed to speak truthfully and wisely. The rabbit fur on the end of the stick reminds him that his words must come from his heart and that they must be soft and warm. The talking stick could also be called the 'listening stick.' This is all about taking 100 percent responsibility—whether you are the speaker or the listener."

Stu nodded, soaking it all in. "That's all well and good for the Native Americans, but . . . I can't go waving a talking stick around in a conference room or in a meeting with one of my sales managers."

"Why not?" Alfred asked patiently, barely stirring on his side of the park bench.

"Well, for one thing, they might beat me over the head with it when they hear what I have to say . . . but, for another, it's just not very practical."

"I agree, Stu, but you can have a mental 'talking stick.' For instance, as the speaker you can ask questions that indicate you're ready to stop talking and start listening."

"Like what?"

"Well, for instance, you might say something like, 'What do you think, Brad?' Or even, 'How are you feeling about this idea, Rachel?' The point is to not just mentally, but also verbally, hand over the 'talking stick' to the next person. Do you see how that might work, Stu?"

Stu started to open his mouth, then chuckled. "I see what you did there, Alfred."

"What's that?"

"You used a question to pass over the talking stick. You asked me, 'Do you see how that might work?'—which now gives me the opportunity to grab the stick and start talking."

Alfred winked. "You're a fast learner . . . and that's no surprise to me. Being patient and listening to the person you are communicating with will help you uncover that person's purpose, so you can bring your purposes into alignment."

Stu nodded, and then instinctively looked down at his watch.

Alfred responded, "I know, we only have a few minutes left. But I have one more important task for you."

Alfred again flipped open the green binder and found Listening Aid 6, which was labeled, appropriately enough, "The Significant Six." He resumed his line of conversation. "Here is an exercise to help you understand the importance of taking 100 percent responsibility."

Stu looked at the page with curiosity.

Alfred explained, "In the left-hand column, write the names of the six most important people in your life—these are the people to whom you should be listening. Then consider how these six people would rate you as a listener on a scale of one to 100, with 100 being the very best listener and one being the worst—and write your expected scores in the center column."

Stu gave a quizzical glance, just as Alfred tipped his wrist up to check his own watch.

"We have time," Alfred said. "Let's do it right now."

Stu got out a pen and quickly went to work. On the page, he wrote six names and six numbers.

Take 100% Responsibility

The Significant Six

1. Identify the top six people to whom you should be listening (spouse, boss, kids, co-workers, friends, etc.), and write their names in the spaces provided.

2. On a scale of 1 to 100, how do you think each person would rate your ability to listen? In the left column, estimate the rating you expect to receive from each person.

3. On a scale of 1 to 100, how does each person rate your ability to listen? Ask each person to rate your ability to listen, and write their scores in the right column.

People to whom you should be listening	On a scale of 1-100, how would this person rate your ability to listen?	
	Expected Score	Actual Score
1. Jennifer	50	
2. Carl	45	
3. Rachel	40	
4. Brad	35	
5. Charlie	65	
6. Linda	75	

Consider:
- How did your actual scores differ from your expected scores?
- For each person, what is the cost of a low score?

©2012, Dr. Rick Bommelje   **LISTENING AID #6**

When he completed the task, Stu looked up and asked, "What do I do now?"

"As you look at the people and the scores, what are some conclusions you can make?"

Stu sighed blankly and shook his head.

Alfred clarified. "Many people say that the people who are most important to them in life would rate them the lowest. When I ask them, 'Why do you think this is?' the response often is, 'I guess I'm too comfortable with them, and don't think I have to constantly pay attention to my communication effectiveness with them.'" Alfred paused. "Do you think this is true for you?"

Stu was still uncertain of how to respond. He held up his expected scores to show them to Alfred, and said, "I don't know. What do *you* think about my scores on the Significant Six?"

Alfred studied the scores and said coolly, "If you were in school, you would be failing all subjects."

"Thanks," Stu said sarcastically. Then he grinned with resignation and added, "I agree ... these scores have got to change."

Stu examined the card again, and then reluctantly asked, "So ... there's another step in this exercise?"

"Yes," Alfred said.

"Do people really do this? Ask the 'significant six' to provide actual scores?"

"Well," Alfred said with some hesitation, "not everybody does it."

Stu blinked, and gave a heavy sigh. "That's a relief," he said. "The idea of getting that kind of feedback from people sounds . . . well, kinda scary."

Alfred nodded in assent. "Yes, it does."

After a moment of silence, Stu glanced up again. Softly, he added, "But it also sounds like an important thing to do."

"It is important," Alfred stated. "But like I said, not everybody does it. The people who follow through on that extra step are the ones who are serious about taking 100 percent responsibility."

Alfred waited silently; he could tell his student was deep in thought.

Stu nodded as he carefully put the listening aid back inside the folder. Mentally, he made a promise to himself. *It won't be easy, but it's time for me to step up and start taking responsibility. In the next week, I'm going to speak to Jennifer and Linda about how they would rate my listening. After I get some feedback from them, then maybe I'll be ready to talk to the others.*

Alfred waited until he thought Stu was ready to hear him. "The Significant Six provides you with a great opportunity. I challenge you to go directly to these people, ask them how they would rate you as a listener, and have them tell you why. Then be ready to SIER* . . . because they will be giving you golden advice.

"The responses you get from your significant six will help you identify the specific benefits you achieve when you intentionally take full responsibility as a sender and a receiver. And—if you are open to SIER*ing their ideas—your significant six will also help you identify the specific *costs* that occur when you *fail* to take 100 percent responsibility."

As he patted Stu on the shoulder, he added, "I know it sounds scary, but after you've done it, you'll be so glad you did. When you meet with your significant six, just remember: these people care about you. And in asking them to rate your listening, you'll show that you care about them."

Alfred checked his watch and stood up from the park bench. "Time to stop for today," he said. "I think we've both got other appointments waiting for us."

"Thanks, Alfred," said Stu, shaking hands with his mentor and friend. "And, again, I'm sorry I was late."

"No worries. It's not the mistakes we make that count; it's how we learn from them that really matters," Alfred said. "I have one more thing for you."

Stu looked up to see Alfred reaching over to present him with the talking stick.

"This is my gift to you," Alfred said.

"Really?" Stu asked.

Alfred nodded and smiled.

With surprise and gratitude, Stu took hold of the stick. In doing so, he felt a pronounced duty to hold himself 100 percent responsible for his communication.

CHAPTER 15
Ditch the Distractions

Stu was in his car, waiting at another red light, when his mobile phone began to chirp. Stashed inside the car's cup holder, the phone skittered and danced with each vibrating tone. *It's probably Linda . . . making sure I'm on my way.*

He took his right hand off the steering wheel to reach down and grab the buzzing device. As he did, he glanced up briefly—the traffic light was still red. On his phone was a text message: *Conference room reserved and ready for your 1 pm meeting with Carl. Where are you?*

A quick look at his dashboard clock; it was 12:45 p.m. and he was just a few blocks away from the office. With his hands resting on the steering wheel, he used his thumbs to write back to her: *Just picked up a surprise for Carl, will be there in a few.*

As the light turned green, he placed the phone back in the cup holder, and gently reached over to the passenger seat to ensure that the fancy gourmet bakery box didn't slide onto the floor. He took a deep breath. The "new car" smell that had built up from weeks of regular detailing was now replaced by the aroma of fresh-baked cookies. Stu knew that Carl's weakness was his sweet tooth; this thoughtful gift was sure to please the boss at their one o'clock meeting.

Not more than a minute later, the phone buzzed again. Stu waited until he was stopped at another red light to see Linda's next message: *Three-month progress check-in! Please be on time.*

Stu chuckled at her motherly concern; it caused him to recall the stern message Alfred had given him only a week earlier about taking 100 percent responsibility for his actions. He began punching in his reply to her: *Do not worry.*

Stu heard a honk behind him, and he looked up to see the light had turned green. He took his foot off the brake and tapped the gas pedal. He continued typing out his message: *I won't be late.*

But as he hit the "send" button, the call of a wailing siren made him drop his phone. In the rearview mirror, he saw flashing lights. He immediately scooted over to the side of the road to give the right of way to whatever it was—an ambulance or fire truck—that obviously needed to get around him.

Unfortunately, the siren and flashing lights followed him to the curb.

He checked his rearview mirror again. A uniformed officer stepped from a police car and approached Stu's driver's side window.

"Can I help you, officer?" Stu asked, trying to smile.

"License and registration, please," said the officer. Though he appeared relatively young, the tone of his voice indicated that he meant business.

Stu slid out his license, plucked his registration from its hiding place in the driver's side visor, and handed them over. He looked at the clock; it was 12:51, and he was only two blocks from the office.

"May I ask why you stopped me?" Stu asked.

The policeman slid his mirrored sunglasses down the bridge of his nose. "You are aware it's illegal to text while driving, aren't you, sir?"

"I wasn't technically *driving* when I started texting," Stu sputtered. "I was at a red light, and when it changed I was just finishing up. . . ."

"Your car was moving while you were texting, sir. I'm going to have to write you a ticket."

Stu wanted to groan, but he held it in. *Obviously this kid does everything by the book.*

He thought the officer would write the ticket at his window, peel it off, and send him on his way. Instead, the young man strolled back to the police car, got in the driver's seat, and carefully filled out the paperwork.

Stu watched the time tick by on his dashboard clock. He used the time to send Linda one more text message: *Stopped temporarily, tell Carl I'm on my way.*

Finally, a full fifteen minutes later, the officer stepped out from his car, walked up to Stu's window, and handed over the ticket. "Sir, there's a reason why texting while driving is against the law. The bottom line is, it's dangerous. You're four times more likely to get into a serious crash when you're texting. If that text message just can't wait, do everybody—and yourself—a favor, and park your car before texting."

Stu took the ticket and gave the young man an insincere thank you. As he pulled back into traffic, he glanced again at his dashboard clock. It was 1:12 p.m. Stu consciously resisted the urge to screech his tires as he pulled away from the curb.

When he finally arrived at the office, he ran into the building carrying his laptop bag and the box of baked goods. He was out of breath as he rounded the corner of the hallway in front of Conference Room D. He was just close enough to catch Linda's soothing voice coming from inside, saying, "He told me he was on his way!"

Stu recognized the second voice as well. "Unbelievable! He knew how important this meeting was," Carl growled.

At that moment, Stu popped in through the open doorway. Linda gasped in surprise, then shouted, "Oh, here he is!"

"I was on my way here with more than enough time when I got stopped by a cop. I texted Linda to let you know I was running late. Did you get the message? I was looking forward to this meeting—so much that on my way here I picked up some of your favorites. See? Cookies from Monk's Gourmet Bakery."

Linda, clearly feeling the sudden tension in the room, slipped discreetly past Stu and sped down the hall.

Carl's face was expressionless, but he eyed the bakery box carefully.

Then he shook his head and glared. "Stu, I'm flattered that you remembered my favorite cookies. I really do appreciate the attention to detail in at least *one* area of your performance, but . . . you're twenty minutes late for our meeting."

"Look at the time on the ticket, Carl," Stu insisted, placing the bakery box within reaching distance and sliding the yellow copy of his ticket across the desk.

"The fact that you were speeding here only tells me you were late to begin with."

"But I *wasn't* speeding, Carl," Stu blurted helplessly. "I was ... um . . . texting."

Carl opened his mouth to speak, then decided against it. Instead, he stood, silently. Ignoring both the crumpled ticket and the tempting box of baked goods on the conference room table, he strode purposefully toward the door.

"But what about our meeting?" Stu asked helplessly as his boss paused in the doorway.

"I've wasted enough time waiting. The unfortunate part of this whole thing is that I wanted to come here and commend you on the good reports I've gotten from your team lately. But their praise notwithstanding, it's *me* you need to impress, not them. And based on what I'm seeing today, it looks like nothing much has changed."

"So . . . my status?" Stu asked hopefully.

"You're still on probation. You have three months to go before your next performance review. I suggest you use those three months wisely."

• • •

Several hours later, Stu and Alfred sat on matching red chairs outside a downtown ice cream parlor.

"Why the long face today?" Alfred asked. "I thought you liked ice cream."

Stu gave Alfred a glance and a half-hearted smile as he took an absent-minded bite of butter pecan. *Alfred is making an effort to engage in social communication . . . I guess I can return the favor.*

"I do like ice cream . . . thanks for treating. And, of course, thanks for agreeing to see me at the last minute like this."

"Well," Alfred admitted, "I must admit you sounded pretty frantic when you called today."

"I don't want to be frantic, but . . . it's just that, I thought I was doing so well. And now as far as Carl is concerned, I might as well be back where I started."

"Is that what Carl said?" Alfred asked, a knowing tone to his voice.

Stu thought for a moment. "Um . . . not exactly," he said ruefully, the pout on his face revealing his true emotions.

"Well, what did he say?" asked Alfred, settling back into his chair as the evening sun bathed his face in a warm glow. "Why don't you tell me about it?"

Stu took a breath as he sorted out his thoughts.

"It all started with today's meeting. It was a big one; my three-month 'midterm,' as Carl called it . . . kind of a test run for my six-month review. Anyway, I was all excited, because you and I had been doing such great work together. I even left work over lunch to pick up Carl's favorite baked goods for the meeting. Anyway, that's where the trouble started."

"You got the wrong kind of muffins?" Alfred joked.

"Cookies," Stu corrected.

"Oh . . . you got the wrong kind of cookies?" Alfred teased. A broad smile spread across his face and his eyes twinkled, and Stu couldn't help but relax and let out a little laugh.

"Okay, well . . . I wish that was the extent of it," Stu said, finally easing into the conversation. "No, it was on the way back from the bakery that I got stopped by the police."

"Oh," Alfred replied. "I hope you weren't speeding because you were late."

"That's just the thing," Stu said excitedly. "I was running ahead of time because of what I learned from my last lesson with you. I was absolutely taking 100 percent responsibility for my actions by giving myself plenty of time to get back to the office before the meeting."

"So what was the problem then?"

"I got stopped for texting while driving! Can you believe that?"

All of a sudden, Alfred's face changed dramatically. It appeared to Stu that one second, Alfred was his usual, cheerful self; the next second, his jaw muscles clenched and he turned away to avoid Stu's eyes.

"Alfred? What's wrong?"

The older gentleman took a moment to collect himself. "Nothing's wrong," he finally said, forcing a smile. "It's just that, your story reminds me of something that happened in my neighborhood. It was about two years ago; a teenage boy was texting while driving, and he ran through a red light, hitting a mother and her two little girls as they crossed at the signal. The young mother was seriously injured, but she lived. The two little girls died . . . it was tragic. Can you imagine the grief that woman carries with her today?"

"I heard about that," Stu said, suddenly feeling chilled at the memory. *What enormous loss and sadness were caused by a teenager's foolish mistake.*

"It was some teenager without a clue, right? Some mixed up kid . . . ," Stu offered.

"He was sixteen," Alfred said quietly, still looking down at the ground. His voice had lowered an octave. "Stu, I'm surprised at you."

Stu hung his head as well, not quite in shame, but in understanding. "I was actually at a red light and when I took off I was watching the road the whole time." As he heard himself saying it, he knew it was a weak defense.

"You had to look down to send your text message, didn't you?" Alfred asked. "And type? And receive?"

"Yes, but . . . only for a second."

Alfred blinked and shook his head. "That's what that young man kept saying at the scene of the accident. 'I only looked down for a second' . . . a second is all it takes when you're distracted."

Alfred reached over to reassure Stu with a pat on the shoulder. "Listen, you didn't come here for a lecture and I don't mean to scold you. It's just, as someone who got a second lease on the miracle that is life, I'm sensitive to these things, you know?"

"I understand," Stu said gently.

"Well . . . it's probably time for us to get started," said Alfred, changing the subject to a lighter topic. He pulled an orange folder out of his bag and slid it over to Stu. On the outside was a printed label that read, "Ditch the Distractions."

"What's this?" Stu asked.

"It's this week's lesson," Alfred smiled.

"But . . . I was just expecting to talk. Isn't our lesson scheduled for later this week?"

"That's true, but clearly you're in need of this right now. After all, what is texting . . . what is your mobile phone while you're driving, but one big distraction?"

"Okay, sure . . . but . . . I'm not sure I understand your point. I *was* listening. I mean, maybe it wasn't the right place to text . . . but I was listening while I was texting. I heard the siren right away, didn't I?"

"Ah," Alfred said, narrowing his eyes and putting his hand up to his chin. "Now we get to the heart of the distraction. You might have had your *ears* open, but you weren't really paying attention because your mind was focused on texting. You were doing what we call 'fake listening.'"

"Fake listening?" Stu asked, surprised.

Alfred explained. "When you are *really* listening, you are fully engaged. That's what SIER* is all about. There is really no such thing as 'fake listening'—you are either engaged in SIER* or you're not. If you're not, then you are disengaged. So it's like a light switch: you're either in the on position, or the off.

"Distractions are everywhere and waiting to capture our attention. Like your mobile phone today . . . you may not see it as a distraction, but it is. A distraction is anything that interrupts SIER*. However, we all have the power to reduce or eliminate distractions in order to focus on top priorities. This is why it's important to master this week's strategy, 'Ditch the Distractions.'

"The key to ditching the distractions is to understand and apply the focus of control," Alfred explained. "There are some distractions you can control, and some you can't. The challenge is to deal with the things you definitely can control."

Here Alfred looked pointedly at Stu. "One of the things you can control, Stu, is when to text, and when not to text."

"I guess that's true sometimes," Stu countered. "But . . . I mean, in my job, I have to—"

Alfred held up his hand. *"All the time,"* he interrupted. "Tell me, would you text during an important sales meeting, with a client sitting right across from you, sleeves rolled up and ready to negotiate?"

"No, of course not. That's prime selling time. But, I mean . . . "

"Every distraction takes away from how well you're listening."

Stu nodded; he could see Alfred's point now.

Alfred continued, "There are also two types of distractions that you face: *internal,* or things that are in your mind, and *external,* which are things in your environment. Examples of external distractions would include all of the noises that you listen to."

"You mean . . . like a phone?" Stu suggested.

"Or a radio, a television, or background music," Alfred nodded. "Or even other people's conversations when you should be focusing on your own. There are as many distractions as there are ways to be distracted.

"The biggest challenge is to try to convert the things that you believe you can't control into things that are controllable. For example, let's imagine that you're in a business meeting, and the building operations manager comes in and tells you that they're going to be testing the fire alarm system. A few minutes later, the alarm goes off as you are trying to conduct your meeting. But it doesn't go off for a few seconds; it rings and pulses continuously. Even with a distraction like that, you have choices on how you deal with it.

"You can remain in the room, aware that there is no danger, and continue with your meeting. Or you can suspend the meeting and go outside until the noise subsides. You do have control over your actions because you have control over your thoughts. Unfortunately, many people become victims of their own distractions."

"I can see how that might happen," Stu confessed, "particularly in light of today's events. So, I know I'm easily distracted. What am I supposed to do about it?"

"Well, the first step is to identify the distractions that you deal with on a daily basis. Start with external distractions; they're the easiest to identify. What types of distractions do you deal with on the job? Things such as a ringing telephone, walk-in visitors, room temperature, noises of all types, the speaker's voice and the way he or she looks, and your vibrating mobile phone, just to name a few.

"For dealing with external distractions, like noises in the environment, it is important to shift things into the category of things you can control. So while you may not be able to control the noises, you can control the way you respond to them and think about them. This becomes a very important exercise in self-discipline and self-leadership. You must police yourself and control the numerous and constant distractions in your life. If you don't, the distractions will control you. It's as simple as that."

"But how do I do that?" Stu asked, suddenly feeling less than confident.

Alfred smiled and put his hand on Stu's shoulder. "You'll get the hang of it over time. You have to get to a place in your life where you not only recognize an external distraction, but know how to overcome it."

Stu frowned; Alfred sighed. "Look around you. We're on a busy sidewalk, with kids running around, traffic a block away, horns honking, people talking, phones ringing, and yet you're managing to hear every word I say and, what's more, focus in on it. So ... how do you manage to block out all those external distractions now?"

"That's easy," Stu grinned. "I'm motivated to listen to you because if I don't, I'll lose my job!"

"Okay then," Alfred smiled back. "Maybe you should just pretend that every conversation you have for the next three months is a use-it-or-lose-it proposition. That way you'll have to ditch the external distractions."

Stu looked uncertain, but he conceded that Alfred had a good point. *If I could ditch the external distractions once, I could learn how to do it again—and again and again. It would be like everything else Alfred suggested: a habit I have to regularly force myself to adopt.*

"Now," Alfred moved on, "internal distractions include daydreaming; jumping too quickly to conclusions about a speaker's statement; engaging in mental arguments while the speaker makes his point; and any emotions that you have, such as joy, excitement, anger, anxiety, or attraction. Each distraction that you have can result in some type of cost, especially if it is repeated over and over. The opportunity is to create a specific plan to overcome your internal distractions.

"For example," Alfred explained, "one way to raise your awareness is to wear a rubber band around your wrist. When you detect any type of internal distraction, simply snap the rubber band and force yourself to come back to the moment. After all, you're in charge."

"The rubber band sounds like a good idea," Stu admitted. "But are you sure that I need it? I can be having a conversation and make lists in my head at the same time . . . I'm good at multi-tasking."

"Multi-tasking?" Alfred yelled in mock anger. "Don't get me started! On second thought . . . let's talk about multi-tasking."

"Okay," Stu said, surprised to see Alfred so animated.

"Many people pride themselves on how many tasks they can handle at the same time and believe that they are excellent multi-taskers. Dr. Grove was really big on this point. He said that multi-tasking is a myth. Multi-tasking is a term taken from the computer field. But computers don't do multi-tasking; rather, they do something called 'task-switching'—doing one task at a time, but very quickly. The same thing happens with humans.

"The mind can manage only one thought at a time. So when you're talking on the phone, checking your email messages, and trying to respond to your boss's requests—all at the same time—something is going to be ignored. It is crucial to slow down when going through the SIER*ing process; or, in other words, you need to slow down to go faster."

"Wait," Stu interrupted. "How's that? Slow down to go faster?"

"Yes," Alfred said. "By doing one task at a time and giving each task your full attention, you'll get the tasks done more efficiently and effectively. When you try to do multiple tasks at the same time—and one or more of those tasks requires you to listen—you are much more likely to miss key information, ask people to repeat themselves, or do an incomplete job. You wind up having to go back and fix mistakes that you made because you weren't fully paying attention, and your efforts turn out to take more time in the long run."

Stu nodded in acknowledgment.

"Let's take a look at this. There is a listening aid in your folder that shows you."

Alfred waited while Stu reached into his folder to find Listening Aid 7: "Listener's Attention Patterns."[3]

"There are five listening patterns, four of which are negative and create mistakes, and one that is most effective. The dotted-line arrow represents a message that is being sent, while the solid arrow represents the listener's attention.

"In the first pattern, you see a small departure in the listener's attention. The listener is staying right with the speaker, but you see that after an extended period of time there is a small lapse. In other words, the listener goes out for a short period of time; yet returns quickly. This is the most effective pattern that there is, because you come back. You beat the distraction."

Here Alfred paused and smiled. "This is the pattern you are in right now, Stu."

"Really?" Stu asked.

Alfred nodded, continuing, "In the second pattern—the tangent—the listener starts out with the best intentions but quickly goes off for an extended period of time. We can assume that the listener eventually returns sometime later . . . or maybe he doesn't. This pattern can create a cost because while you are 'out,' you may miss some valuable information.

Ditch the Distractions

Listener's Attention Patterns

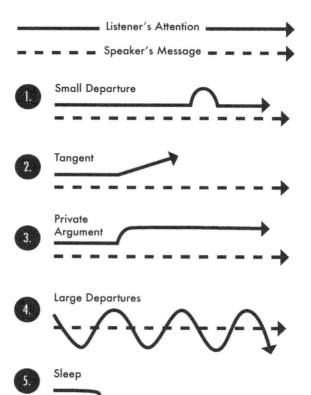

LISTENING AID #7

"In the third pattern—the private argument—the listener is challenged by the speaker's message in some way. Maybe he disagrees with the point that is being made. Instead of paying attention, the listener begins to prepare a defense in his mind. When the speaker completes her message, the listener launches into defending his own point of view. The problem with this pattern is that while the listener is debating in his mind and preparing his defense, he is missing valuable information from the speaker that could help him understand the speaker, and perhaps better inform his own position. So this is another negative pattern.

"The fourth pattern shows a series of large departures. In this one, the listener is 'out' more than she is in. She is simply not paying attention to the speaker in the moment, though she thinks she is because she comes back periodically—though briefly each time. This pattern can produce a significant cost because the listener is relatively unaware of what is going on around her.

"The fifth pattern is when the listener is zoned out so much that he actually falls asleep."

Stu laughed. "I've seen this one in some of the meetings at work."

Alfred paused to take a sip of water before asking, "So, which pattern do you think you use most often?"

Stu looked down at the card, mentally scrolling through Alfred's lesson. "I would have to say I spend a lot of time in the third pattern, what you called a 'private argument.' Especially in my leadership role, I'm so busy thinking about how I'm going to correct my sales managers, I have a hard time staying with their point all the way to the end. I know that's what most of them complain about, anyway. I do that one in my personal life as well."

Alfred nodded sagely before adding, "Well, that's why we're here; applied knowledge is power. And the challenge, of course, is to stay in the first pattern as much as you can. Doing this will help you to ditch the distractions. Since distractions are so widespread, it is unusual to see action taken to control or ditch them.

"Finally, the main point is to tolerate no distractions. The way to do this is to focus on one thing at a time—and to know what matters most. I know this idea is simple to understand, yet it's difficult to implement. As Dr. Grove often said, the word 'focus' serves as an acronym: '**F**ollow **O**ne **C**ourse **U**ntil **S**uccessful.' I know you can do that. You're good at keeping your head down and staying in the race."

Alfred stood to indicate that he needed to be on his way. The two men said their goodbyes, genuinely thanking each other for the time spent in each other's company.

Long after Alfred was gone, Stu sat and pondered the lesson. He looked at the card on the little ice cream parlor table and traced his finger along the varying lines, imagining his attention going out the window with each lined departure. Then he looked out across the sidewalk, suddenly tapping into all the external distractions he'd managed to tune out while Alfred spoke. He smiled weakly, realizing how difficult it was going to be for him to ignore those distractions day in and day out, for the rest of his life.

For years, I was known as the guy who said "take me to the challenge." I was ready for anything, and I thought I could conquer the world. When this listening journey started, I approached it with the same determined attitude. But it feels different this time; instead of conquering the world, I've got a much greater challenge: conquering myself.

CHAPTER 16
Lead Your Emotions

Stu smiled as he saw the long line of cars pulling into the downtown hotel. Once inside the parking garage, he patiently traveled up several levels to reach an open parking spot. *What a great crowd this year! I'm happy to take a longer walk to the convention center if it means we'll have plenty of talented candidates to choose from.*

Seeing a throng of people waiting for the elevator, he decided to take an alternate route to the hotel's convention center. Colorful signs were placed strategically along the walkways. At the large convention hall, huge banners welcomed everyone to the 11th Annual Wallsey Community Job Fair. For Stu, being at the convention center brought back fond memories. *I'll never forget the first time we came to this job fair, just a few years ago. I built a great team at the Wallsey branch when I managed it. Too bad Brad is struggling to keep it together.*

Once inside, he found the grand hall bustling with energy. Booths were arranged row upon row, with the logos of numerous businesses competing for attention. The crowd was a mix of modern professionals; men and women of all ages, sizes, and races. They were dressed professionally as well; slacks and blazers for the men, stylish suits for the women. While many were on the young side—freshly scrubbed college graduates and MBAs—others were middle-aged and distinguished looking.

Stu spotted the DynaCorp booth at the far end of one of the alleyways. He craned his neck over the crowd in an attempt to find a familiar face. He had heard that several members of his former team would be on hand to meet and greet. But as he came closer to the booth, he saw only two people he recognized. Maureen Brock, one of DynaCorp's human resources managers, was dressed in her usual conservative navy blue suit as she spoke to a mature gentleman in a striped tie. A few yards away, Brad Chappelle, sales manager of the Wallsey branch, was looking his handsome best as he gave his business card to a tall blonde in a tight skirt. *Brad asked me to get more involved, so I hope he appreciates me being here. With two open positions to fill, he can certainly use the help.*

"Hey, you made it!" Brad said as he turned to greet Stu.

"Yeah, looks like we're packing them in this year," Stu replied, raising his voice to be heard over the noise.

"Yeah, it's good," Brad said. "I've gotten a bunch of new resumes."

"I was expecting some folks from the team to be here helping you out. Aren't Kylie and Mac coming today?"

"I told them not to," Brad said. "We've got too much going on right now."

Stu took a moment to process what he had just heard. *You told them not to . . . ?*

"Excuse me," Brad said. "I've got people waiting." He paced over to introduce himself to a pair of pretty young ladies who were standing nearby, admiring him.

Stu fumed. *The job fair is supposed to be a team effort, with everyone pitching in to represent the company. How are we supposed to make a good impression with only three people?*

"Stu?"

His train of thought was interrupted by one of Dyna-Corp's longtime HR managers. "Hi, Maureen," he said, giving her a quick hug. "How do you think it's going?"

"I'm glad you're here," she replied. "I thought we were a little short-handed."

"I can see that." he replied.

"Let's get you a nametag!" she said, reaching under the table to pull out a company-branded adhesive badge and a marker. "It's going well, and there is plenty of interest. With you here maybe we can get to more people." As she spelled out Stu's name, she motioned toward Brad, who was still chatting with the two young ladies. "It seems like Brad is selective about who he talks to," she said.

"He's young," Stu said absent-mindedly.

Maureen captured Stu in her steady gaze as she pasted the nametag onto his chest. "Well, I hope he's got the best interest of the company in mind," she said. "And I hope *you* do, too."

A small group of attendees had gathered a few feet away, waiting for their turn. "Excuse me, are you with DynaCorp?" one of them asked.

She walked over to greet them. "Hello, I'm Maureen Brock. Nice to meet you."

Stu set his notebook down under the table and jumped into the fray, greeting applicants, shaking hands, and gathering resumes. As the time ticked away, he observed Brad in action. *He spends ten minutes at a time talking to one girl, while Maureen and I move from one person to the next trying to get as many leads as possible. She was right; the kid is treating this like his own private singles mixer.*

When there was a lull in the action, Stu took the opportunity to pull Brad over to a corner of the booth. "Let's talk for a minute," he said.

"I'm glad you could come," Brad said in his own carefree way. "We're having a great turnout today, don't you think?"

"I have seen a lot of potential candidates," Stu said. "How about you?"

"Definitely," Brad enthused. "I've already scheduled five callbacks for next week."

"You've got five callbacks scheduled?" Stu asked suspiciously. "I don't think I saw you talk to more than five people since I got here."

Brad's smile retreated. "Well, I was here for a full hour before you arrived. What are you saying, exactly?"

"I'm saying that we've got two open positions to fill at your branch, and we need to meet as many people as we can." Stu could tell that his tone was starting to rise; he tried to compose himself as he continued. "Let me say that again; we need to meet as many *different* people as we can."

Brad squinted in confusion. "You think I'm not meeting enough people?"

"You're not listening to me. I said *we* need to meet as many *different* people as we can," Stu replied. "And since you brought it up, I was expecting to see some people from the team here today, to help pick up the slack."

"Who? Kylie and Mac?" Brad sneered. "We don't need their help."

"I think you do." Stu's tone was rising again. "They're the two best people you've got left."

"I know you think they're great because *you* hired them," Brad said with an edge in his voice. "But I need them *selling* today instead of spending their time here."

"Okay," Stu said. He realized that the tension of the moment was getting the better of him; he decided to take a new approach. "Let me be more specific. It looks like you are spending a lot of time with just a few people. Wouldn't it make more sense for you to meet as many people as you can?"

Brad's face went blank. "I thought that was why you and Maureen were here . . . to meet people and help collect the resumes."

"That is why we're here, but . . . " Stu was losing his patience with the conversation. *I'm just not getting through to him.*

Stu let loose. "I think the issue is that you're spending too much time flirting with the single girls, when you're supposed to be focused on finding talented candidates."

Brad took a moment to look Stu over, then he responded in kind. "I'm offended that you would think I'm just here to 'flirt with the girls,' when what I'm trying to do is follow your direction to manage my own team and find solutions on my own. But while we're talking about how I spend my time, why don't we talk about how you spend yours? I thought you were here to help with the job fair, not to critique my recruiting skills."

"I didn't intend to critique anything," Stu said defensively. "Until I saw you ignoring good candidates."

"I can't talk to everybody here!" Brad rankled. "I'm not ignoring anybody. I talk to every candidate who comes up to me." He let out a heavy sigh, then continued with his rant. "Do you just want to make the hiring decisions for me? Because I thought *I* was the manager of this branch, and that I could hire who I want."

"Absolutely; of course you should hire who you want," Stu said. "But don't come complaining to me because the people you hire can't perform like seasoned pros."

"Is that what this is really about?"

"What do you mean?" Stu asked.

Brad continued with a calm defiance. "It seems like it's always about *the seasoned pros* for you. How many times do I have to hear about how you took the Wallsey sales team and turned them into a 'powerhouse'? About how the way *Stu* did things was *right*, and how the way *I'm* doing things is *wrong*? About how I'm screwing up *your team* ..."

"I never said that," Stu replied. *Even if I did think it ...*

"Well this is my chance to build *my team*, and I've got some ideas for what kind of talent we need. But you never want to hear about those ideas because it might mean that your powerhouse team wasn't so great after all."

"I think you need to stop right there." Stu interrupted.

"I will in a minute, I've got one more thing to say," Brad continued. "I've talked to quite a few people around this company, and I hear all the time that you weren't that great of a manager when you started, but you were given time to grow into it because Carl was patient with you. I wish I was reporting to a manager who could work with me the same way that Carl worked with you. Is there some reason why I don't deserve the same treatment?"

Stu could feel the heat coming off of his face. A moment passed while he stared at Brad. *How dare he talk to me like that! If we weren't in a room full of people, I would let him have it!*

Brad finished up his argument. "I'm sorry, but ... that's just the way I see it."

Their private conversation was interrupted when Maureen approached them with a concerned smile. "It looks like we have a few more people waiting to talk to us," she said.

Stu turned back to Brad. "I tried to give you some simple feedback, and you can either use it or ignore it," he fumed. "I can't tell you how to run your branch; all I can do is measure your performance. If things don't turn around at the Wallsey branch, I guess we'll have our answer."

"I guess we will," Brad said.

Stu picked up his notebook from under the table and walked over to shake Maureen's hand. Summoning up some forced pleasantness, he said, "It was great seeing you today! I'm going to let you and Brad finish up here." Without waiting for her response, he walked out of the booth and past a small group of waiting candidates. Then he pulled off his DynaCorp nametag, tossed it into a nearby wastebasket, and moved quickly toward the exit.

• • •

Stu was still steaming about the interaction with Brad when he got to his car detailing session later in the week, and he couldn't hide it. By the time Stu finished telling his story, Alfred had already started working on the chrome hubcaps.

"Sounds like you're a little peeved at Brad," the older gentleman smirked.

"You think so?" Stu had to smile at Alfred's understatement. "Okay . . . I suppose I'm a little worked up about it. But can you blame me? This kid's messing up the team that I put together. It's pissing me off."

"Why is that?"

"I just can't help but believe that he's headed toward some bad hiring decisions because he's focusing on the wrong criteria and overlooking good people. He doesn't even appreciate the people that he has—people who have the kind of experience he should listen to."

"A-ha!" Alfred boomed, slapping the car's bumper. "So the Wallsey team was performing perfectly when you started managing them?"

"No, they needed direction," Stu replied.

"But they all stayed during your tenure. Nobody left?" Alfred asked.

"We had some turnover, but that was necessary to get the team right."

"Oh," Alfred said, nodding. "So all of the people hired were experienced and ready to go when you hired them?"

"Not entirely, no. I mean, Brad's in his twenties and I hired him. But it was a calculated risk and he was very, very qualified," Stu said. "Okay, so where are you going with this?"

Alfred continued polishing the headlights happily as he smirked. "I think you're more like Brad than you care to admit."

"How's that?" Stu asked, intrigued.

"Well, I think the reason you're so frustrated with Brad is that he's trying to do the same thing that you did, but you don't like it. When you started as a manager, you had to hire new people, manage them, coach them, and give them time to grow together into a team. It sounds like Brad is trying to do the same thing—he's trying to build a team that works for him. But when he tried to explain this to you, you shut him down because you think he's trying to undo your work, and maybe you're taking that personally, a little bit."

Alfred paused for effect, then continued. "Brad did try to explain this to you, did he not?"

Stu couldn't help sounding like a spurned schoolboy. "Well, he tried to."

"Tried to?"

"I didn't really hear what he said . . . I kind of stormed out on him."

Alfred chuckled knowingly, standing and stretching out his legs before reaching into the back of his van for Stu's latest folder, a red one this time.

"Stormed out, huh?" Alfred asked, leaning against the back of his van as Stu rifled through several pages of various notes inside the folder. "Doesn't sound like a very healthy way to listen, does it?"

"The thing is," Stu argued, "I went there to *really* listen to Brad. I mean, do you think I wanted to spend half my day at a job fair? Hardly! But once I got there, the more I saw, the madder I got. I guess, well, I guess my emotions ran over my better intentions."

Alfred nodded, almost seeming pleased.

"What are you smiling about?" Stu asked.

"Nothing. It's just, well . . . your experience with Brad at the job fair couldn't have been a better introduction to this listening lesson. That's because today we're talking all about leading your emotions. It's one of the most important and difficult strategies to master."

Stu let out a heavy sigh. "Is it even possible?" he asked.

Alfred grabbed a cotton cloth and began buffing the hood of the car. "Of course it's possible. It's just not very easy. Let's go back to the job fair, and Brad, and how you lost your temper because you held an opposite view on a topic. Were you able to listen effectively to anything that was said after you saw what Brad was doing, and you made up your mind that he was wrong?"

Alfred didn't wait for Stu to respond before continuing.

"Now consider a time when you failed to listen carefully, simply because of your emotional reaction to the speaker. Maybe you disagreed with their political position or religious beliefs. Maybe you disliked their age, gender, or ethnicity. At what point did you stop listening? In every case, your emotions got in the way.

"Because your emotions affect everything you do, it is important to take a broader look at your *triggers*. A trigger is anything that sets off an emotional reaction. Dr. Grove said that emotional triggers can cause internal reactions to speakers, topics, and word choices. That emotional reaction disrupts your effectiveness as a listener. And your emotional triggers aren't only negative; they can also be positive or neutral."

Stu took out his notepad and started writing. Then he looked up to notice Alfred smiling at him. "I know," Stu said. "I do it all the time now." *I'm sure Alfred remembers when I said that taking notes was a waste of time.*

"We'll start with positive triggers," Alfred continued. "You know that you hold positive emotional views for certain people, topics, or sensations. When you are not aware of the power of such positive emotions, your listening becomes lazy. When you are emotionally connected to the speaker or the topic, or the way it's delivered, you may not bother to hear the complete message."

"How do you mean?" Stu asked.

"Well, as you listen to your favorite subjects, or to someone you like, or to voices that appeal to you, you enter your 'emotional happy place'—whether you realize it or not. You may get a positive emotion from a person's physical appearance, or by certain words that suggest powerful emotional images. These triggers provoke positive emotions in you that put your listening ability at risk; your "feel good" emotions bias your listening so you may not get the message. Without awareness, positive emotions can lead to ineffective listening habits."

Stu nodded. "I see . . . sort of like young lovers who can't see each other's flaws . . . or an activist who is driven by a political message without seeing all sides of the issue."

"Good examples," Alfred said. He waited a moment for Stu to look up from his notes, then continued. "Neutral emotions also lead unknowing listeners to tune speakers out. While being neutral may provide an objective listening position, it can also be a trap. As emotionally neutral listeners create a position of disinterest, they simply drift out of the listening process. Effective listeners overcome the counter-productive impact of neutral emotions by identifying them. In the process, your focused listening interest and activity will be heightened.

"Dr. Grove used to emphasize that poor listeners lose emotional control in one or a combination of three specific areas: *speakers, words,* and *'hot' topics.* Once they are confronted by a person who upsets them, or hear a certain word, or consider a topic that riles them up, they react. The effect is usually negative."

"It certainly seems to be," interjected Stu.

"In your case, with Brad, I think you likely experienced all three. For one, even though you went to the job fair with the purpose of helping Brad, I know from previous conversations we've had that you've been frustrated with him. So, good intentions or not, you were likely pre-programmed to have a negative reaction to him. Then, maybe even predictably, Brad started making word choices that sent your emotions into overdrive: words like 'my team' or 'your team.' These words spilled over into discussing a 'hot' topic that finally pushed your emotions over the edge: Brad's perceptions of your hiring decisions, and your perceptions of his."

Stu nodded, amazed at Alfred's insight.

"Some people quickly turn the reaction into anger, like you did. And any negative feelings and emotions toward the *speaker, topic* or *language* will totally interrupt the listening process. In worst-case scenarios, negative emotions often lead to a refusal to listen. In addition, any attempt to listen with negative emotions usually results in angry listeners, and the evidence is clear: *mad listeners are bad listeners.*

"The challenge is for you to be able to identify what the triggers are and then put things into slow motion so that you can go through the steps of the SIER* process: Sense, Interpret, Evaluate, and Respond, with Memory connecting the steps together.

"It's like when you 'count to ten' to keep from getting mad. Let's put it into the language of listening. What you are really doing when you count to ten is putting a space, otherwise known as 'the golden pause,' between the S-I-E and the R—a pause between your evaluation and your response. When you do this, you will be better able to control your emotions, and ultimately, respond in a way that you choose. When you are able to do this consistently, you will develop a powerful habit that will give you the edge in dealing with others."

Stu nodded. "I could have really used this tactic with Brad."

Alfred laughed quietly. "Well, now that you have it, you'll never be able to use that excuse again, will you?"

"I suppose not," Stu admitted.

"There are three simple steps that can help you lead your emotions in a positive way."

Stu returned to his note-taking.

Smiling, Alfred continued, "Step one is to identify your triggers—the words, people, and hot topics that create a strong emotion in you. You do this by observing yourself in the moment. Remember, the emotion can be positive, neutral, or negative. Then figure out why these triggers have an effect on you. Think hard about this and identify exactly why these words, people, and hot topics cause your emotional reaction.

"Step two is to anticipate triggers in your conversations. Once you have identified your triggers, you'll know what you're looking for and you should be able to see the triggers coming. This lets you prepare yourself for times when you will encounter your triggers, so you can decide the response you prefer."

"I think I do that," Stu said.

Alfred raised a questioning eyebrow.

Stu clarified. "What I mean is, I can usually see the triggers coming. I could probably do a better job of choosing a more effective response."

"Even after you have prepared for the triggers, you still have one more step," Alfred said. "Step three is to practice gaining self-control through disciplined thought. You do this by staying in the moment, and by answering the question 'Is it of value?' before you say or do something. Ask yourself, 'Is what I am about to say or do of value to the other person?' If the answer is no, then you know it's time to remain silent."

Alfred waited until Stu looked up from his note-taking; then he asked, "If you had paused and asked 'Is it of value?' in your conversation with Brad, would you have withheld some of your comments?"

Stu thought for a moment. "I probably shouldn't have accused him of flirting with the girls."

Alfred opened his eyes wide, and blinked. Then he reached into his red file folder, pulled out Listening Aid 8, and handed it to Stu.

"Here's Listening Aid 8, which can serve as a quick reference for you."

Stu thoughtfully studied the listening aid.

"Remember, Stu, you have the power to lead your emotions if you choose to. If you want to make a positive difference, it requires doing things that may seem difficult at first. These concepts are simple to understand, but the challenge is to use them consistently. So, the goal is to *intentionally respond* rather than *unintentionally react* to what you listen to."

• • •

In the weeks that followed, Stu redoubled his efforts to practice leading his emotions. He did his best to keep his attention in the present, and to respond rather than react. It wasn't easy work for him, but with each passing day, listening became more comfortable and natural for him. And as he changed the way he communicated with others, the people around him changed the way they perceived him.

Lead Your Emotions

Three Steps to Lead Your Emotions

1. Identify your emotional triggers.
   - Mentally observe yourself in the moment.
   - Gain more knowledge about the people, topics, and language that trigger your emotions.
   - Label the triggers as positive, neutral, or negative, and determine why they are so.

2. Anticipate triggers in your interactions.
   - Prepare yourself mentally to encounter triggers.
   - Decide the preferred response.

3. Practice gaining self-control through disciplined thought.
   - Intentionally interpret before making a judgment.
   - Remind yourself that you decide your response.
   - Before you respond, ask yourself: "Is it of value?"

©2012, Dr. Rick Bommelje   **LISTENING AID #8**

CHAPTER 17
Take Meaningful Action

Stu arrived at Riverview Park and pulled into the same parking spot he had used just a few weeks before—the one near the water fountain, in the shade of an old elm tree. There were no other cars in the lot, and as far as Stu could tell, no other people in the rest of the park. He had the entire place—scenic and peaceful as it was—to himself.

Checking his dashboard clock, he saw that he had twenty minutes before Alfred's arrival was expected. He reached into his bag and pulled out his notebook; then he got out of the car and found a comfortable seat on a park bench.

Taking in a long, deep breath, he surveyed the scene around him. The park was beginning to show more signs of life. A pair of joggers trotted past him on the sidewalk nearby. An older woman from the neighborhood waved at him as she walked her golden retriever. All the while, water danced and trickled through the fountain, providing a soothing sound in the background. *What a beautiful place to relax and reflect.*

Stu opened his notepad and thumbed through the pocket to find the first card Alfred had ever shown him, the Listening Pays framework.

With an unhurried attitude of appreciation, he thought about his experience with each of the strategies. *It took me a while to build a solid foundation . . . learning how to SIER* was like learning a new language. And I didn't know how many bad habits I had until I started practicing the healthy listening habits. I always wanted to blame others for communication breakdowns, but I can't do that now that I take 100 percent responsibility.*

Suddenly, Stu looked up. From out of the sky, a pair of brown ducks flew over him to land with a splash in the fountain. He took another deep breath and observed the scene around him. Nearby, a young mother was pushing her baby in a stroller. He looked down at the card again. *Ditching the distractions isn't always easy, but when you start doing it, you see the benefit of keeping your attention fully engaged, much like I'm doing right now. And leading my emotions is probably one of the hardest things I'll ever have to do, but it's going to make a huge difference in my relationships.*

Stu looked down and read the last of the six strategies: Take Meaningful Action. *I'm not sure what Alfred has planned for this lesson, but I'm ready to take it in.*

The sound of an engine got Stu's attention. He looked up to see the D'Amato Detailing van pulling up next to his car. At his own leisurely pace, Alfred got out and walked over to the park bench, carrying a yellow folder.

Stu stood up and greeted his mentor with a handshake and a pat on the back.

"Well, we finally made it," Alfred said. "Our last lesson."

"Yes," Stu said, smiling.

"How do you feel about it?" the older gentleman asked.

"Proud of the progress," Stu said sincerely. "A little sad to think this is our last one."

"It's not the last time we're going to meet," Alfred said reassuringly. "We still have several more auto detailing sessions scheduled, and we can continue to talk about your listening efforts. But, yes . . . today's lesson is the last of the six strategies."

"Before we get started," Alfred said, "I want to tell you how proud I am of you . . . not only for all of the improvements you made, but for simply sticking with it and making it to this point."

"You're proud of me for just being here?" Stu asked, grinning.

"Yes!" Alfred said as he chuckled. "You don't know how many people give up along the way!"

"I can understand the temptation to quit," Stu said. "But I didn't believe I had a choice."

"More people should have the good fortune of getting their jobs threatened," Alfred said.

Stu laughed out loud. *Alfred has such a unique way of looking at things. But he's right; I probably wouldn't have*

LISTENING PAYS

Achieve Significance
through the
Power of Listening

Six Strategies

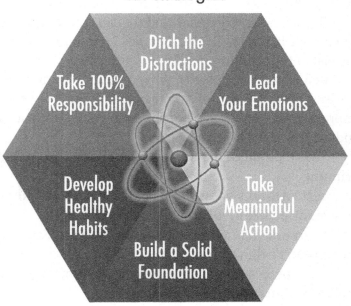

©2012, Dr. Rick Bommelje

started on this journey otherwise. And here I am today, grateful for the ultimatum.

Looking Stu in the eye, Alfred smiled as if he could read the younger man's mind. They both nodded in acknowledgement.

"Well, shall we get started?" Alfred asked.

"I'm ready," Stu replied.

The two men sat down on the park bench. Alfred reached into his yellow folder and handed over Listening Aid 9, a card with a strange symbol on it.

Stu looked at it carefully. "Why is it in Chinese?" he asked.

"Dr. Grove said the Chinese people have really captured the spirit of listening with this symbol," Alfred explained. "The Chinese written language doesn't make use of a phonetic alphabet like ours does; instead, each word is represented with a visual symbol or collection of symbols, and each symbol has meaning. So this shows us that for the Chinese, listening involves four parts: ears, eyes, the selfless act of giving undivided attention . . . and having an open heart. You recall that when we started, we talked about how Dr. Grove described listening as SIER*ing—using all of our senses. He said that we must listen with our whole bodies."

Stu took a moment, and then nodded. "I've certainly learned that lesson. During these past few months, I think I've developed a much deeper awareness of my own listening strengths and weaknesses—as well as those of other people."

"How do you mean?" Alfred asked.

Take Meaningful Action

Chinese Symbol for Listening

TO LISTEN = TING

 EARS

 EYES

 UNDIVIDED ATTENTION

心 **OPEN HEART**

©2012, Dr. Rick Bommelje   **LISTENING AID #9**

210

"Well, I watch the people I communicate with. I notice how they react and respond to me, and to others around them. The more I learn and practice the strategies, the more I see errors in other people's listening behaviors. It doesn't matter who they are—store clerks, CEOs, or just strangers on the street; it seems like few people bother to listen to each other anymore!"

"That might be," Alfred said knowingly. "But I would guess that you're also noticing these things because your own skills have improved."

"I know that's true," Stu replied. "In fact . . . something happened just yesterday that made me think of this."

"Oh?" Alfred raised an eyebrow.

"Yeah," Stu continued. "I was planning an out-of-town business trip—a visit to one of our big clients that was thrown together at the last minute. I was on the phone with our corporate travel agency. I explained to the woman on the other end of the line that I went online to get information about the flight I wanted, but I had to book it over the phone to get the corporate rate. She asked me what flight I was interested in, and I answered, 'I'd like to book the flight at 3:03 p.m. this coming Tuesday from Center City to Chatsworth.'

"She goes away for a moment, and I'm thinking that she's checking the rate for the flight. When she comes back, she asks, 'What day was that again?' So I repeat my request. Then she asks me, 'And that was from Center City to . . . where again?' She goes away for another moment, and when she comes back, she says, 'Sir, did you try checking the availability for this flight online?' In that moment, I thought of you and your favorite saying: 'Listening pays in many ways . . . because you make the investment.'"

"And why did you think of that?" Alfred inquired.

"Because . . . she was violating the strategies, and there was a cost," Stu said. Without any prompting, he continued. "First, she failed to build a solid foundation—she certainly wasn't SIER*ing. She had some gaps in her listening habits—I don't think she was paying genuine attention or taking notes. And she didn't take 100 percent responsibility; it was like she wanted me to do all of the work for her!"

Alfred gave a knowing look that communicated his pride. "And . . . what was the cost for that ineffective communication?" he asked.

Stu took a moment to think. "Well, the short-term cost was that repeating everything was taking up extra time. And the long-term cost was that it created a loss of trust in her and the travel agency. Yeah . . . unfortunately, she wasn't able to regain credibility with me for the rest of the call."

"Just out of curiosity," Alfred asked, "how did *you* behave during all of this?"

"I think you would have been proud of me," Stu said. "The old me would have gotten upset with her for wasting my time. But on this call, I controlled my anger and led my emotions. I didn't bark at her, or hang up; I patiently repeated myself until the flight was booked. I got what I needed *in spite of her*, not because of her. I also learned—thanks to what you taught me—that I finally had the tools to take responsibility for my own actions."

"I *am* proud of you," Alfred said with sincerity. "When I hear you explain how you've analyzed listening breakdowns—either yours or someone else's—I can tell that you have a top-of-mind awareness of your own listening behaviors. Over these past few months, I've seen you really strive to create value in every relationship—with the people on your work team and, perhaps most importantly, with your wife."

Stu blushed a bit.

"You've made terrific progress, and I would like to acknowledge that with a special assignment," Alfred said.

"Okay," Stu said, a bit baffled about what his mentor intended.

Alfred reached into his folder and pulled out what appeared to be a children's book.

Before he even saw the title, Stu recognized the illustration on the front cover. "*The Tortoise and the Hare!*" he said. "I remember my mother reading that to me as a kid. And it's one of Jennifer's favorites—she reads it to her students."

"I'm glad you like it!" Alfred said. "Dr. Grove shared this story in class, and ever since then, I have made a habit of reading the book every week, as a constant reminder of his teachings."

"You read a children's book every week?" Stu asked in amazement.

"Absolutely! This story is not just for children. It's one of the most famous fables ever written. Aesop wrote it over two thousand years ago, and it's just as meaningful today." Alfred held the book up. "In keeping with today's lesson, I would like for you to read this out loud."

While Stu thought the request was strange, he could tell that Alfred was quite serious.

Alfred passed the book over. With a wide grin on his face, he said, "Read it out loud!"

Stu took the book, opened the cover, cleared his throat, and began to read.

The Tortoise and the Hare
An Aesop Fable

One day a hare was bragging to the other animals about how fast he could run. "I have never been beaten," he said, "for I am the fastest animal in the forest. I challenge any one of you to a race."

As he continued his arrogant boasting, he saw a tortoise standing among them. The hare laughed at the short feet and slow pace of the tortoise.

The tortoise stretched out his long neck and quietly said, "I accept your challenge."

"That is a good joke," said the hare; "I could dance circles around you the entire way." With a hearty laugh, the hare agreed to race the tortoise.

The forest animals met and mapped out the course.

On the fixed day, the race began. As expected, the hare left the tortoise far behind.

About halfway through the course, the hare decided that he had time to take a nap. "I have plenty of time to beat that slow-moving tortoise," he thought. And so, lying down under a shady tree, he fell fast asleep.

As for the tortoise, he never for a moment stopped. He took one good step after another, slowly and steadily plodding along.

Some time later, the hare finally awoke from his nap. "Time to get going," he thought. As quickly as he could, he dashed to make it to the finish line, where he met the tortoise patiently awaiting his arrival.

The moral of the story:
Slow and steady wins the race.

When Stu finished, he closed the book and looked up. He was pleased to hear the story again, and he quietly anticipated Alfred's next direction.

With a kindly smile, Alfred asked, "Do you see any similarities between this story and your own?"

Stu looked down at the book and nodded his head. "Well . . . I think to a certain extent, I can identify with both of these characters." He took a moment to gather his thoughts. Then, he proceeded, "When I started this journey, I was the rabbit."

Stu explained himself with care and deliberation. "I wanted a quick-fix solution, and . . . looking back on it, I was impatient and arrogant. The rabbit's attitude set him up for failure, but he couldn't see how hurtful his attitude was, and he lost the race. I can relate to that, even today. I'm still at risk of losing my job."

Alfred waited patiently for Stu to continue.

"But I can also relate to the tortoise. Even though he was up against tough odds, he persevered throughout the entire race. He didn't give into any distractions . . . he didn't let the rabbit push his buttons . . . and he stayed focused on the goal until he was victorious."

"And how does that apply to you?" Alfred asked.

"Well . . . I've learned so much by going through this process that I know I'm a different person. When I started, I felt like I was coming from behind. I've had my share of setbacks and hard lessons, but I always did my best and didn't give up. My relationship with Jennifer is better than it's ever been. And so . . . even if I do lose my job, it's all been worthwhile."

Alfred's face showed great satisfaction. "Stu, this is exactly how great listeners approach every situation. Everything you said describes what today's lesson—taking meaningful action—is all about." He reached into his folder and took out Listening Aid 10.

Alfred explained, "This lesson could have been presented at the very beginning, the first time we met, to give you a preview of what lay ahead. But I've found that it makes a much greater impact when it is presented at the end, to acknowledge what you have accomplished and prepare you for the work that continues long after the 'lessons' are over.

"Taking meaningful action involves five important stages that occur in a sequence of increasing mastery. I'd like to get your impression of each of these."

Alfred looked at Stu solemnly. "First, you have to commit; decide to change."

Take Meaningful Action

The Sequence for Taking Meaningful Action

COMMIT
Decide to change.

KNOW IT
Open your mind to learn what to do.

DO IT
Apply what you know.

BE IT
Make listening part of your nature.

TEACH IT
Pass the knowledge and strategies on to others.

LISTENING AID #10

There was a pause as Stu thought.

"Yes," Stu said. "You do have to *commit*. I remember before we started, that was one of the first things you said to me: '*First, you have to commit.*' I didn't understand it at the time, because quite frankly, I didn't *want* to commit—I wanted the easy answer. But I see it clearly now. You have to decide to change; this means letting go of old ways, and adopting new ones. It's a tough decision to make."

After another pause, Alfred continued. "Then, you have to *know it*—open your mind to learn what to do."

Stu responded, "Listening—*really* listening—requires you to learn new ideas and new skills. The hardest part of this for me was opening up my mind. I was so set in my ways, sometimes it felt like there was no room in there for something new. And for a while, the old ideas and the new ideas tried to occupy the same space. After a while, the new ideas were stronger than the old ideas, so the old ideas got replaced."

Alfred smiled. "After you know it, you have to *do it*—act on what you know."

Stu didn't hesitate on this one. "Well, this is the real test—practicing everything you know. I think this was the most challenging thing for me, to practice the skills day in and day out. If I hadn't been under pressure to do it, then I think I would have been tempted to give up. But in my case, I didn't have a choice, so I had to figure out how to do it."

Alfred nodded. "So, when you've acted on what you know consistently over time, you can *be it*—you've made the practice of listening a part of your nature."

Stu took a moment to think about his response. "I can see that I've definitely gotten rid of some bad habits, and put new, healthier habits in place. But I also see that I have a way to go before all of it becomes second nature . . . definitely room for growth."

"Of course," Alfred said. "You've only just begun. With continued effort, all of this will become more natural for you." Alfred looked down at the listening aid again. "And the final stage is to *teach it*—you take what you've learned and pass the knowledge and strategies on to others."

Stu squinted and glanced up at Alfred. "Hmm . . . I don't think I've reached the 'Teach It' stage yet. I'm still working on my own listening."

"Do you see why it would be important?" Alfred asked.

"Based on the example you've set for me," Stu said, "I'm sure I'll be ready to do that when the opportunity presents itself."

Alfred nodded. "Teaching others how to listen accomplishes a number of things. It keeps the concepts fresh in your mind, and it also reminds you to constantly set the example. But most importantly, it lets you help others become more effective communicators." Alfred paused a moment, and then asked, "I think you're ready for this next step, because you have grown so much over the past few months. Is there anyone on your team who would benefit from better listening?"

"I'm not sure," Stu replied. "I'll have to give that some thought."

• • •

Stu's day of reckoning was finally at hand.

Though he was ready to accept the decision no matter what it was, he still felt a great deal of apprehension. As he drove into the office, his heart was beating in his chest, and his mouth had gone dry. His level of anxiety surprised him, since earlier that morning he had taken a two-mile jog. *Running usually settles my nerves, but not today; maybe a half-marathon might have worked better.*

He knew the decision had already been made, and there was nothing more he could do to sway Carl one way or the other. Nevertheless, he was committed to being a professional. He was wearing his best suit—the tailored one, freshly cleaned and pressed.

As he came into the office, he headed straight for Conference Room D, the "intimate" room where Carl preferred to hold his one-on-one performance evaluation meetings. There was a chair at the head of the table, which he left open for Carl. Taking the seat next to it, he unbuttoned his jacket but left it on. He wasn't sure if this would be a long meeting or a short one.

Stu looked at his watch and noted that he still had five minutes before the meeting was to begin. *Carl might fire me, despite six months of constant forward motion, but at least I showed up early for the meeting.*

A few minutes later, Carl came into the conference room carrying a large manila envelope labeled "Stu Preston—Personal and Confidential." He walked up to Stu and formally extended his hand, offering a sincere greeting. "Thank you for coming today . . . and being on time."

Stu rose out of his chair to shake Carl's hand. He had no words for replying; instead, he merely took a breath and nodded his head.

"You look sharp," Carl said.

Stu cleared his throat. "Thanks . . . well, today is a big day," he rasped.

"Is it?" Carl asked, as if he had forgotten the purpose of the meeting.

"I'd say so," Stu said solemnly. "I mean . . . my future hangs in the balance. I've been waiting to hear this news for the past six months."

Carl nodded and held his hand up to scratch his chin. "Hmm . . . I suppose so."

Stu could hardly believe his ears. *In all of the scenarios I had imagined—from cracking open a bottle of champagne to being escorted to the exit—I would not have imagined that Carl would overlook the importance of this meeting.*

At last, Carl grinned and said, "Oh, Stu . . . your job's been safe for the past two months."

"What?" Stu breathed a sigh of relief. Then he stammered, "How come you never said anything?"

"That's my fault, and I'm sorry," Carl replied. "I shouldn't have made you wait all that extra time. But I was so impressed by your growth, I wanted to see how far you could take it."

"I'm happy with the decision," Stu said. "I couldn't imagine leaving DynaCorp."

"I couldn't either!" Carl said. "That's why I'm glad that you turned things around."

"Thank you, Carl," Stu said. He reached out to shake his boss's hand again.

Carl motioned to the empty chairs. "Please, we have some time . . . let's talk about it."

They both took their seats.

"I'm curious about something," Stu started. "At my three-month review, you said you thought that nothing much had changed. You mean I pulled it together in the past three months?"

"At the three-month mark, I knew you had made some progress, but you still had some room for improvement. Arriving late to that meeting and trying to bribe me with cookies didn't help."

Stu looked down with a half-smile, embarrassed to remember his behavior from that meeting.

Carl continued, "But when I look at you now, I see a changed man. I've heard good reports from your team, and what's more, your sales numbers have been up for the last four months in a row."

"I'm glad you've noticed," Stu said. "I've been more focused on my people than on the numbers."

Carl's smile returned. "That's what I mean. Your whole emphasis has shifted."

"I've been working at it," Stu said.

"I want to hear about that," Carl said. "What did you do to work at it?"

"Well, it all goes back to what you said six months ago—listening. That's what you asked me to focus on when you called me on the carpet for in your office. Remember?"

"Of course," Carl said. "Listening was one of the things you were neglecting at the time, along with people skills, attention to detail, and your sales numbers."

"But that's just it," Stu said excitedly, leaning forward. "I learned that it *all* comes back to listening. When you listen to your people, *really listen* to them, the results follow."

Carl sat back and nodded.

Stu continued. "I can't take all the credit. I was fortunate enough to meet someone who coached me these past six months."

"Who coached you?"

Stu hesitated a moment, uncertain of how to explain it all. "His name is Alfred D'Amato. He's a fascinating guy . . . he overcame a hearing disability and went to school to study communication. I met him out here in the parking garage."

"You mean . . . Alfred?" Carl inquired. "The guy who washes the cars?"

"Yes, the auto detailer," Stu said, showing his esteem. "He really gave me the gift of listening."

"Hmm . . ." Carl intoned, taking it all in. "Well, however you got it done, the results have been amazing.

I'll have to say hello to Alfred the next time I see him in the garage."

Carl looked at his watch and then stood, indicating that it was already time for him to get going to his next appointment. He pointed at the envelope resting on the table. "The details are all in the report, if you're interested. Let me know if you have any questions." Then he leaned in and looked Stu directly in the eye. "And, just for the record, you've been making me look good lately. So . . . I consider the pact unbroken."

Stu straightened up in his chair and gave Carl a smile. "So do I," he replied.

Carl gave Stu a thumbs-up as he exited the room.

Stu opened the envelope and quickly read the evaluation he'd been hoping for—working for—for the past six months. He was gratified by the words, and the anxiety associated with all of the work now seemed an afterthought.

As he packed the report into his bag, he stopped and pulled out his notepad. Reaching into the pocket, he grabbed the listening aid that Alfred had given him at his last lesson. As he studied the card, he realized that he'd been doing what Alfred had taught him all along: he'd been taking meaningful action.

Stu went through each of the stages in his mind.

COMMIT: My commitment started when I decided to change, and it continued for six long months. Meeting Alfred that day in the parking garage had been a blessing, but I now realize it was the work I did myself—independently, away from Alfred—that was so vitally important.

KNOW IT: Once Alfred showed me what to do, I had the knowledge I needed to achieve my ultimate goal of keeping my job . . . and my marriage.

DO IT: It wasn't always easy, but the more mistakes I made, the more I learned how to overcome my weaknesses and enhance my strengths.

BE IT: Walking into the meeting with Carl today, there was nothing else I could do but be myself. I've made the ongoing effort to replace bad habits with healthy ones and to really listen to the people around me. Fortunately, Carl realized how much of an asset I am . . . and so did I.

TEACH IT: I've still got an opportunity to teach what I've learned to others. I agree with what Alfred said during our final lesson . . . I'm ready to take this step.

Stu put the card back into his notepad and packed up his things.

The moment he arrived at his office, his assistant Linda walked in with two cups of coffee.

She seemed surprised by his arrival. "That didn't take long," she said, wearing an expression of unconditional support.

Stu sighed and picked up one of the coffees. "Really?" he asked. "It felt like six months to me!"

"I meant the meeting," she said.

"I know what you meant," he said in a teasing tone.

"So? What's the verdict?" she asked.

He motioned with his coffee cup for her to sit down in the chair across from his desk.

Linda sat down anxiously, her wide eyes following him as he moved to his chair.

Take Meaningful Action

The Sequence for Taking Meaningful Action

COMMIT
Decide to change.

KNOW IT
Open your mind to learn what to do.

DO IT
Apply what you know.

BE IT
Make listening part of your nature.

TEACH IT
Pass the knowledge and strategies on to others.

©2012, Dr. Rick Bommelje   **LISTENING AID #10**

Stu sat contentedly and smirked at Linda's angst. "Don't worry," he said gently. "I'm not going anywhere."

"Oh!" she yelped, jumping up. She stepped over to hug him. "I knew you could do it! I knew all along."

"You did?" he asked, returning the embrace.

She pulled away and looked up at him with a smile. "Well . . . I'm glad that you did it."

"Yeah," he said, remembering her initial concerns. "That's what I thought."

They spent a few minutes chatting in his office, sharing the satisfaction of the moment. When they were done, Stu put the evaluation report in the file with his previous performance reports. Within a few hours, the high emotion of the morning faded away and the work returned to a steady—though newly revitalized—routine.

As Stu drove home from work that night, his mind was still busy. Rather than congratulating himself for saving his job, he was focused on what to do next. *At our last lesson, Alfred said that the work continues long after the "lessons" are over. I've got an opportunity to take this even further.*

Epilogue

The three of them stood in the driveway, next to Alfred's white van. "It's very nice to meet you," Alfred said, reaching out his hand.

"I've been waiting a long time for this," Jennifer replied, grasping his hand with a soft but friendly grip. "I've heard so much about you, I feel like I know you."

"I've heard great things about you, too," Alfred said.

Stu was beaming, his happiness apparent to both Jennifer and Alfred. *This introduction has been long overdue.*

"I'm gonna get us some cold drinks," Stu said, excusing himself. "I'll be back in a minute." He went back inside the house, passing through the open garage door.

Alfred and Jennifer exchanged smiles.

"I don't know if Stu told you this or not, but it was only a couple of weeks ago—the night of our anniversary—that we made a toast in your honor," she said.

"No, I didn't know that," Alfred said.

She stepped forward to touch his arm. "I want to thank you," she said, looking at him intently. "The work you did with Stu made a huge difference . . . not just for him, but for me, too. I really mean it . . . we communicate on a whole new level now. And I've never seen him happier."

"I noticed the change while he and I were together," Alfred said. "But I think you need to know . . . Stu did all the work. He really cares about you."

Jennifer smiled at Alfred, her eyes shining.

"Here we go," Stu called. He returned carrying two bottles of lemonade and some napkins.

"I'll let you two get on with your business," Jennifer said. "I'll be back a little later." She walked into the house, giving Alfred one more look of affirmation.

"She's wonderful," Alfred said as he opened up his lemonade.

"I know, I'm a lucky man" Stu said, grinning.

"So you have a new car for me to take care of?"

"Yes," Stu said, "right over here." He led Alfred to the other side of the van, where a new Mercedes sedan was parked.

"This is yours . . . or Jennifer's?" Alfred asked.

"It's mine," Stu stated matter-of-factly. "I traded in the Porsche last week. But this car works out better for both of us."

"How so?"

"Well, for the past few months, we've been commuting together at least once a week. It's not that far out of my way to take Jennifer to the school, we save some money, and it lets us spend more time with each other. Besides that, we decided we were ready to get a family car."

Alfred nodded and glanced over at him, but Stu continued.

"Anyway, there's another reason I wanted to meet with you today," Stu said. "I told you that I was awarded Sales Director of the Year, right?"

"Yes . . . congratulations, you earned it," Alfred said.

"Thanks," Stu said, obviously still proud of his accomplishment. "But there's more to it than that. Each year, DynaCorp puts together a corporate conference, and they invite some of the award winners to share best practices. They've asked me to be one of the seminar presenters. I think this is an opportunity to achieve significance, and I could use your help."

• • •

The convention center was buzzing with DynaCorp employees, all dressed in business casual attire and wearing large name badges. The crowd was mostly managers and executives, but there were also a number of hourly employees in the mix.

With only ten minutes left before the end of the mid-morning break, attendees carefully made their way to the sessions of their choice. Inside one of the meeting rooms, about forty-five people had assembled for a seminar entitled "Listening Pays." Outside the door of that meeting room, Stu and Alfred greeted guests as they entered.

As the hallways started clearing out, Stu turned to Alfred. "Are you nervous?" he asked.

Alfred could tell that it was Stu who was nervous. He tried to put his friend's mind at ease. "Not at all," he said. "The rehearsal was smooth; we have a good crowd and a powerful message."

"I agree," Stu said.

Suddenly, Linda poked her head through the door. "Stu, we need your help with the audio."

"I'll be back in a minute," Stu said, leaving Alfred outside the door.

The older gentleman continued greeting the few remaining attendees as they filed in.

The hallways were just about empty when the doors of the other meeting rooms began to close. Alfred checked his watch—it was time to begin. He turned to release the doorstop when a tall young man strode up to him. "Is this the listening session?" he asked.

"Yes, it is," Alfred said.

"You must be Alfred . . . Stu told us all about you. I'm Brad Chappelle."

"I *am* Alfred. It's very nice to meet you, Brad."

The two men shook hands.

"I've been looking forward to this session," Brad said. "I know you spent a lot of time working with Stu, and it really helped him be a better manager."

"I enjoyed it," Alfred said. "Both of us benefitted from our time together."

"Well, I just wanted to tell you that Stu and I have been meeting regularly to go over the material you provided, and I'm learning a lot. We just finished up healthy listening habits, and now we're working on taking 100 percent responsibility."

"I hope you're getting value out of it," Alfred said, smiling until his eyes crinkled.

"I am," Brad said.

Stu walked up to tell Alfred that it was time to head inside.

"Good luck, guys," Brad said as he left to take his seat.

They closed the doors and the noise in the room settled down to an expectant murmur. As Stu and Alfred looked out into the crowd, they saw a sea of interested, inquisitive faces.

Stu moved to stand at the front of the room and welcome the group. "Some of you may be wondering— *why in the world are we having a listening seminar*?"

The crowd—especially those who knew Stu well—let out a friendly laugh.

Stu continued. "A year ago, I would have been wondering the same thing. But now, as a result of what I experienced, I know that *listening* is the reason behind my region's improvement in sales performance. I didn't do it alone; I had a strong team. But I also had the help of this man, my mentor, Alfred D'Amato."

Alfred stepped up to join Stu at the front of the room. "Thank you," he said. With a polished, measured delivery, he charmed the audience. "It's an honor for me to be standing next to Stu Preston today. I'm proud of what he and his team accomplished, and I can tell you—from first-hand experience—listening pays . . . "

ENDNOTES

Chapter 8

1. Adapted from the 10 Golden Rules. Steil, L. and Bommelje, R. (2004). *Listening Leaders: Ten Golden Rules to Listen, Lead and Succeed.* Edina, MN: Beaver's Pond Press
2. SIER* created by Dr. Lyman K. Steil Steil, L., Barker, L. and Watson, K. (1983) *Effective Listening.* New York: McGraw-Hill College

Chapter 15

3. Adapted from Coakley, C. (1993). *Teaching Effective Listening: A Practical Guide for the High School Classroom.* Auburn, AL: Spectra, Inc.

ABOUT
RICK BOMMELJE
(BOMB-L-J)

Many refer to him as the "Listening Doctor," although he calls himself the "Listening Student." Rick Bommelje has more than thirty years of professional experience in leadership, management, and adult education. He is a faculty member in the Department of Communication at Rollins College in Winter Park, Florida. Rick was selected as one of the top 300 college professors by the Princeton Review.

Rick is a past president of the International Listening Association and was inducted into the Listening Hall of Fame in 2011. With a master's degree in management and a doctorate in educational administration, and advanced leadership study at Harvard University and Northwestern University's Kellogg School of Management, he specializes in the development of listening and leadership behaviors.

Rick has been serving professionals in organizations in the areas of leadership and communication development since 1977. Over the years, his courses, seminars, and workshops have benefited thousands of leaders from an impressive list of organizations worldwide including: Olive Garden Italian Restaurant, Dow Jones & Company, Orange County Public Schools, Whirlpool Corp., Siemens Shared Services, Walt Disney World, AT&T, U.S. Army, Lockheed Martin, Certified Slings, Inc., Lake County Schools, Coca Cola Bottling Company, Lynx, Department of Defense, Hong Kong Broadband Network, Western Digital, Marriott Corp., Tupperware, Dimension Data, and many others.

The appeal and effectiveness of Rick's programs are found in his practical and "real world" approach to education and development. His informal delivery style focuses on practical and substantive content that offers participants immediate and measurable benefits. Dr. Bommelje and Dr. Lyman Steil have authored the pioneering book *Listening Leaders: The Ten Golden Rules to Listen, Lead, and Succeed.*

MEET THE "REAL" ALFRED

ALFRED MARINO
Listening Leader

Alfred Marino is a Certified Professional Concours Detailing Specialist, the highest level of car detailer in the field, and has been mentored by some of the finest nationally recognized Concours judges. His extensive experience, along with a bachelor's degree from Rollins College (Winter Park, Florida), has allowed him to provide his clients with the "educated difference" in professional automotive detailing.

Alfred lost his hearing from German measles at the age of three and regained it when he was forty-one years old after receiving a cochlear implant. While pursuing his degree in organizational communication, he focused on developing his listening and leadership skills as a student of Dr. Rick Bommelje. Since graduating, he has delivered listening workshops with Rick at a wide variety of organizations including Dimension Data, Inc., Northrop Grumman Corp., Lake Co. (FL) Public Schools, the Association of Legal Administrators, Tupperware Brands, and Harcourt-Mifflin-Houghton.

MEET THE "REAL" DR. GROVE

DR. LYMAN (MANNY) STEIL, CSP, CPAE
The Ambassador of Listening

Dr. Lyman K. (Manny) Steil, CSP, CPAE, is internationally known as "The Ambassador of Listening" and a "Speaker Worth Listening To." For more than 48 years, Dr. Manny Steil has helped millions of individuals and a multitude of organizations throughout the world impact their performance, productivity, profitability, and pleasure through enhanced listening and leadership. He is the architect of the STEIL S.I.E.R. model of Listening.

Dr. Steil was the founder and first President of the International Listening Association; author and co-author of four books and numerous articles; creator of the first Effective Listening Video Program; and architect of the award winning Sperry Listen Project. In addition, Dr. Manny Steil has earned the CSP (Certified Speaking Professional) and the CLP (Certified Listening Professional) designations, and has been inducted into both the National Speakers Association "Speakers Hall of Fame" and the ILA "Listening Hall of Fame." Dr. Steil was named as the International Listening Association's 1st "Listening Legend" recognizing those who have made an indelible mark on advancing listening and the ILA. In 2012, he received the ILA's highest award, the Lifetime Achievement Award. Dr. Steil's and co-author Dr. Rick Bommelje's pioneering and award winning book, *Listening Leaders: The 10 Golden Rules to Listen, Lead, and Succeed,* was published in 2004. Dr. Steil is CEO and Chairman of the International Listening Leadership Institute, President of Communication Development, Inc.; former Chairman of the Speech Communication Division, Department of Rhetoric, University of Minnesota and former Director of Debate, Macalester College.

LISTENING **PAYS** RESOURCES

There are a variety of products and services to assist you with your listening development. These include:

- LISTENING PAYS APP
- LISTENING PAYS BLOG
- LISTENING PAYS WORKSHOP & SEMINAR
- LISTENING COACHING
- LISTENING BEHAVIOR ASSESSMENT
- LISTENING PAYS ON-LINE COURSE

FOR INQUIRIES, PLEASE VISIT

www.ListeningPays.com
Dr. Rick Bommelje
Leadership & Listening Institute, Inc.
8530 Amber Oak Dr.
Orlando, FL 32817 USA
407-679-7280
Rick@ListeningPays.com

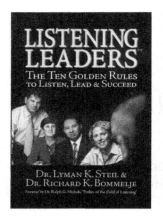

Listening Leaders: The Ten Golden Rules to Listen, Lead, and Succeed is based on more than 50 collective years of Dr. Steil's and Dr. Bommelje's combined work with listening leaders throughout the world. In addition, insightful "Golden Nugget" experiences, drawn from more than 100 "Golden Circle Listening Leader" interviews will help you enhance your ongoing listening and leadership success.

Listening Leaders provides practical answers to such important questions as: What is listening leadership? Why is listening the most important skill for leaders? What separates the outstanding listening leaders from less accomplished leaders? What are the leadership costs/rewards of ineffective/effective listening? How can you become a better listening leader? How can you build a high performance Listening Organization?

When you embrace and engage the priceless rules of highly effective listening leaders you, and everyone you lead, will profit in extraordinary ways. As you listen and lead on you will make everyday count!

"This is the most significant book ever written on listening and leadership, and will profit leaders at all levels in all types of organizations and enterprises."

—Dr. Ralph G. Nichols, Father of the Field of Listening

Order your copy at:
www.ListeningLeaders.com
and
www.Amazon.com

CPSIA information can be obtained
at www.ICGtesting.com
Printed in the USA
LVOW05s0323300717
543135LV00008B/53/P